**Praise for** ...

"This is more than a b... container of magic tr... close to you. From her own humble beginnings, Meredith Heller gorgeously invites us into the creative process of becoming human by learning to attend to and celebrate the full range of our life experiences through the extraordinary alchemy of poetic writing."

— **SARK**, artist, author, and inspirationalist, PlanetSARK.com

"Poetry isn't just art; it's essential medicine. Poetry gives shape to our longing and invites us toward a novel encounter with our deepest and most soulful desires. In this stunning ode to everyone's inner poet, Meredith Heller offers a timely and extraordinary gift to anyone seeking to explore poetic writing. Heller writes, 'I don't really believe that we can teach creativity or poetic writing, but I do believe that we can hone our ability to notice what moves us.' Heller invites the reader to begin with what moves them, however raw and unpolished that beginning might be. And this — to begin — is the bravest and most vulnerable work a poet might do."

— **Danielle Dulsky**, author of *The Holy Wild*,
*Woman Most Wild*, and *Seasons of Moon and Flame*

"This book is perfect for anyone who dreams of writing poetry. In these pages you will find everything you need: tools, examples, prompts, suggestions, and most important, inspiration from a teacher and writer for whom poetry has been a salvation."

— **Jane Anne Staw**, author of
*Small: The Little We Need for Happiness*

"Poetry is language that whispers and shouts and dreams, rants and chants. In *Write a Poem, Save Your Life*, Meredith Heller provides an abundant variety of invitations and open-ended questions so we can translate the truths and textures of our lives into poems. *Write a Poem, Save Your Life* is a guide for teens, teachers, and writers of all ages to write their way into greater clarity and wholeness. Brava."

— **Ruth Gendler**, author of
*The Book of Qualities* and *Notes on the Need for Beauty*

"For anyone who has ever declared, 'I have nothing to say,' Meredith Heller invites you to embark on a brave adventure into the magic of poetry and the tools for finding your truth, lifting your voice, singing your personal song."

— **Sophy Burnham**, author of
*For Writers Only* and *A Book of Angels*

"What an inspiring guide to writing poetry! Meredith Heller weaves her teaching, her prompts, and heartfelt poems into a book that calls all of us to find and celebrate our words. *Write a Poem, Save Your Life* teaches us that through poetry our difficulties can be endured, the unspeakable can be spoken, and both truth and beauty can be shared."

— **Sandra Marinella**, author of *The Story You Need to Tell*

"In her generous, soulful book, Meredith Heller reminds us that happiness is an 'inside job,' that the deepest sense of belonging is to ourselves, and that our own poems can be trusted to take us there. With moving personal stories and inspired student poems, Heller invites us to a banquet of step-by-step tutorials in such life-changing, neglected arts as shape-shifting, ranting and raving, inner shamanism, and so many other 'writes' of passage. I invite young people (and anyone else who'd like to write themselves home) to dive into this curriculum of wonders; it may very well save your life."

— **Prartho Sereno**, prize-winning poet,
Poet Laureate Emerita of Marin County, California,
and founder of the Poetic Pilgrimage:
Poem-Making as Spiritual Practice

"Meredith Heller has written her book *Write a Poem, Save Your Life* with both passion and compassion. She invites everyone to the party, telling us that each of us has a poem and each of us can write it. She follows this up with coaching that is both careful and enthusiastic. Read this book, and you will learn to believe in yourself."

— **Kevin Fisher-Paulson**, author of
*A Song for Lost Angels* and *How We Keep Spinning…!*

"We need poetry in our schools and our lives. Academia places far too much emphasis on 'brain only,' but other modes of learning are essential to well-being. *Write a Poem, Save Your Life* teaches the reader, step by step, how to use poetry to talk about life's struggles, pain, joy, and transformation. It's the perfect resource."

— **Kristi Hugstad**, author of
*Beneath the Surface* and *Be You, Only Better*

"Without rigid rules or tedious tenses, the poet Meredith Heller has written an important, readable book; it is especially useful for adolescents — during their ups and downs. Fortunately, Heller invites everyone to participate in the art/therapy of making poems, to work to formulate their feelings, and to create something that matters."

— **David Bruce Smith**,
founder of the Grateful American Foundation

"During my senior year of college, I took my first and only poetry class, with the poet and professor Hugh Ogden. That class changed my life as a writer and a human being. Hugh passed away a few years ago, so his brilliance is no longer available to the world. *Write a Poem, Save Your Life* is for anyone who wasn't fortunate enough to spend the spring of 1999 with Hugh. It teaches you to love poetry, to write poetry, and ultimately to love yourself. It's a big, heady book filled with lots of tangible, specific strategies to make your poetry come alive in the way Hugh taught me. If you love poetry, this book is for you. If you don't love poetry, this book is even more for you."

— **Matthew Dicks**, author of
*Storyworthy* and Moth GrandSLAM winner

"Meredith Heller invites us to share and speak using words to tickle our fancies and find our own word-ways. Even the table of contents is intriguing. Heller shares her own wending path from disenchantment to depression to the alchemical process of poetry. We hear her move from speechlessness to humming to out-loud song to authentic voice. Heller is vulnerable and inspiring.... She speaks with the truth of a guide who has traveled and continues to travel. She brings us the clarity and simplicity of the poetry toolbox and invitations to write our own perspectives.... Savor every delicious bite of this book!"

— **Wendi R. Kaplan**, Poet Laureate of Alexandria,
Virginia, 2016–2019

"In Meredith Heller's bold new book, she shows us how poetry offers a powerful tool for processing and sharing the joys and pains of being human, as evidenced by her own experiences. Her writing invitations are specific and helpful starting points, as are the examples shared by her students. Poets and writers of all ages and experience levels will benefit from her seasoned, savvy, sage advice!"

— **Rebecca Pollack**, creative writing teacher,
Marin School of the Arts, Novato, California

# Write a Poem,
# Save Your Life

# Write a Poem, Save Your Life

## A GUIDE FOR TEENS, TEACHERS, AND WRITERS OF ALL AGES

## Meredith Heller

FOREWORD BY
SUSAN G. WOOLDRIDGE

New World Library
Novato, California

New World Library
14 Pamaron Way
Novato, California 94949

Text design by Tona Pearce Myers

Library of Congress Cataloging-in-Publication Data

Names: Heller, Meredith, date, author. | Wooldridge, Susan, date, writer of
    introduction.
Title: Write a poem, save your life : a guide for teens, teachers, and writers of
    all ages / Meredith Heller ; foreword by Susan G. Wooldridge.
Description: Novato, California : New World Library, 2021. | Summary:
    "Explores the use of poetry as a tool for self-discovery and emotional
    healing"-- Provided by publisher.
Identifiers: LCCN 2021000475 (print) | LCCN 2021000476 (ebook) | ISBN
    9781608687480 (paperback) | ISBN 9781608687497 (epub)
Subjects: LCSH: Poetry--Authorship. | Self-actualization (Psychology)
Classification: LCC PN1059.A9 H45 2021 (print) | LCC PN1059.A9 (ebook) |
    DDC 808.1--dc23
LC record available at https://lccn.loc.gov/2021000475
LC ebook record available at https://lccn.loc.gov/2021000476

First printing, May 2021
ISBN 978-1-60868-748-0
Ebook ISBN 978-1-60868-749-7
Printed in Canada on 100% postconsumer-waste recycled paper

New World Library is proud to be a Gold Certified Environmentally Responsible Publisher. Publisher certification awarded by Green Press Initiative.

10   9   8   7   6   5   4   3   2   1

To my students and fellow poets,
all us brave ones who write poems to save our lives:

I know you've got a story to tell!
I know there are words curled under your tongue
poems humming in your hands
incantations bubbling in your belly
manifestos in your laughter and love songs in your tears
rants & raves in the swing of your hips
song lyrics spilling out your back pocket;
Let them speak!

Poetry is a life-cherishing force....
For poems are not words, after all,
but fires for the cold, ropes let down to the lost,
something as necessary as bread in the pockets of the hungry.
— MARY OLIVER, *A Poetry Handbook*

# Contents

# Foreword

We all have poems tucked inside, waiting for expression, illuminating the mystery of who we are. In my decades of teaching poetry workshops, I've seen poems of truth and beauty emerge from even the most reluctant writers. "The world is light with my imagination," Kevin wrote in high school, and Aubrey, "I dress myself with rain." A young man in Juvenile Hall wrote, "I'm a brown gangster colliding with death. / I'm a rose slamming love with hate." His poem reveals the rose hiding within his anger.

With wisdom and heart gleaned from her own rocky adolescence, Heller, a masterful guide into the depths of self, provides core questions and invitations that open the way for our souls to speak. "Our poems are our pearls," Heller reminds us. "We take what hurts and make it into something beautiful that has the power to heal us and others." When you "commune with your own being and touch your own truth," she says, "it saves you."

In *Write a Poem, Save Your Life* we are invited to explore all life's experiences, from identity, home, the senses, body language, nature, sex, and death to empowerment, joy, and purpose. Throughout, Heller provides model poems from her students to help guide us.

"Earth rolls into town / like she owns the place" (Riva, 16). "The women are wrapped in the silver of the clouds. Birds fly around their heads, showing the passing of time" (Sophie, 10). *Magic Spell*: "Fang of wolf / and ink of squid / mend my broken heart whole / like when I was a kid" (Izzy, 18).

Understand, it's not the words in this book that will save you, however compelling they may be. It's what these pages encourage *you* to write. Gather your pen and paper and follow Meredith Heller's guidance to write your own poems and save your own life. Join Heller on her quest to help save the world, one poet at a time...

— Susan G. Wooldridge
Author of *poemcrazy: freeing your life with words*

# Introduction

At thirteen years old, disenchanted with society and in search of a deeper truth, I leave home and school and raise myself, living in domes I build in the woods, old barns, and abandoned houses along the Potomac River. I do whatever I can for cash: gardening, cleaning, making jewelry from the dead snakes I find on the road. I teach myself to tan the snakeskin, attach it to a tube of beads I've sewn, and make it into bracelets I sell at a store in town for food money.

I'm kicking around with a free-spirited gang of musicians, experimenting with drugs and sex, testing our edges, all of us desperately wanting to figure out who we are and what we believe in. I watch as my friends go down: overdose, suicide, mental hospitals. Struggling with life-draining depressions I've had since I was child, I often lose my faith. But each time I hit my lowest point, when I no longer care whether I live or die, the poetry comes. The first line is a gift, whispered in my ear; I don't know where it comes from, but I know it's my lifeline. I grab hold of the words, write them down, and then dive in and write, without moving for five or ten or twenty hours, until I've finished a new poem or song. Working on poetry becomes a reason to live, something bigger than me, a way to channel my overwhelming feelings and make something tangible, make beauty from suffering.

At fourteen, I'm brutally raped and beaten by a boyfriend and left for dead. In shock and shame, I crawl inside myself and stop speaking for months. I feel myself dissolving, pulling further and further away, retreating into a dark place where no one can find me. When I'm just about to let go of my life, the poetry comes, and the more I write, the stronger I grow. Naming my pain, I write:

*Clenched Fist*

My head is lead
My heart stone
My body a clenched fist

My lips that once
kissed you
are now cracked
and bleeding
dried-up crones

too bitter
even to
gossip.

Then, finding my voice after months of mute numbness, I write:

## How to Hum

Do you remember
how to listen
to your heart
without crying?

Better yet
how to hum?

It was the high reach
of your voice
that like a rope
you climbed

out of the knotted jungle
through the burnt lung
of night.

When I'm sixteen, my best friend commits suicide. Shocked and heartbroken, trying to make peace with my pain and her passing, I understand that it could have been me. I write:

## Passage of Light

Years after your anger
boiled itself dry

scorching the vessel
of your being clean

I came to understand
that we are the same animal
that our wounding
bleeds the same color

only a different shade
and yours has left you,
softer.

It has not disfigured you
sucking pain to your shoulders
like pins to a magnet

It has not gnawed through
the nerve sheath
leaving you
at its feral edge,
like me

where comfort knows no home
and my name changes
with the passage of light.

A year later, my boyfriend ODs on heroin and burns
down our warehouse. Bereft, I feel the song lyrics for "Little
Boy Blue" coming to me like a gift. I sit all night with my guitar and write until the sun comes up. That night I play it at a

coffeehouse downtown. Writing the song allows me to access my feelings of loss and anger, to begin to accept what feels impossible, and finally, to see that we were both struggling in our own way to grow toward the light. I write:

### Little Boy Blue

Little boy blue
with the hot-wheels tattoo
your hands are empty
your promises few

I read your palm
in the candlelight
I saw how you'd burn me
I saw how you'd die

I'm out behind the firehouse
praying for a sign
sifting through your ashes
I hear them whisper your lines

Up on Danny's rooftop
we watched the full moon rise
you rocked me so sweetly
to the rhythm of your lies

Down in Blagden Alley
where the crooked hookers hung
we grew up like wild weeds
reaching for the sun.

My whole life, I've written poems and songs that saved me. Writing helps me connect with myself, name the feelings that threaten to consume me, pour myself into the deep and meticulous work of crafting a poem or song, and turn my pain into something meaningful. Poetry is a lifeline. Writing is the medicine that cleans out the wound and heals the hurt.

At seventeen, I'd saved enough money from gardening and housecleaning jobs to spend a year hitchhiking through Europe. Everywhere I traveled, I met people like me, people searching in their own ways to figure out who they are, what makes them happy, and what gives them a sense of belonging. I came away asking myself, what can I do with my life that feels meaningful to me? I returned to Washington, DC, passed the high school equivalency exam, and attended massage therapy school, which was how I supported myself for the next twenty-seven years. When I was twenty-five, I started college and worked my way up from remedial classes to honors classes, graduating magna cum laude and receiving a fellowship to the Writing Seminars at Johns Hopkins University. But I found I was still searching for who I was and what mattered to me.

I had a private practice in massage therapy, spinal-cord injury rehabilitation, and health coaching. I worked as a gardener, wilderness guide, and performing singer/songwriter. I managed a retreat center in Hawaii, and I started my own company teaching music and movement classes for children.

One day, while hiking through the woods along the Potomac River, I had an epiphany: if I could get to the kids who were like me, bright and creative, who learn differently, and who don't fit in, if I could help them know their worth and their capabilities, discover their passion and their purpose before they give up on themselves and society, then everything I'd been through would be worth something.

Three graduate schools later, I had found my path. I wove together my passion for writing with my interest in holistic healing and experiential learning. Today I am a California Poet in the Schools, living a life of passion and purpose, doing what I love and helping others find their way. I teach poetry workshops for kids of all ages in both public and private schools — kids with learning differences and health challenges, kids in survival mode at Juvenile Hall, and all the amazing kids and women who attend my weekly poetry workshops on Zoom.

I've heard that we do our best work from the place where we've been wounded. Thirteenth-century Persian poet and mystic Rumi said, "The wound is where the light enters us." Songwriter Leonard Cohen echoed this in his song "Anthem": "There is a crack, a crack in everything / That's how the light gets in." And I say, the crack is also how the light gets out.

On the first day of class, I tell my students, "I'm not here to teach you other people's poetry; I'm here for you to teach me your poetry. Grab your paper and pen, and come outside with me." I ask the kids, "What do you notice? What are you aware of inside and outside you? Take in the quality of the light, the feel of the air on your skin, the sound of the rain, the water droplets balancing on leaves, the color of your friend's sneakers, the tightness in your shoulders, the hunger in your belly, the rhythm of your breath, your sadness, your fear, your desire."

There is a moment of absolute stillness, and then the

shift in energy is tangible. Bodies start moving, smiles break open. It's as if all the kids have gone from being pale crumpled paper bags to colorful inflated balloons. They're breathing, connecting to themselves and the environment, feeling alive and present in their bodies. I ask them to remember five feelings and images as we walk inside and start writing.

I explain that as poets we notice things, feel things deeply, and have a strong need to express ourselves. This expression can be cathartic and empowering. I don't really believe that we can teach creativity or poetic writing, but I do believe that we can hone our ability to notice what moves us. We can develop a love of language and the joy that comes from working to find just the right word and rhythm to convey our feelings. I have found that magic happens when we name our thoughts and feelings, commit them to paper, speak them out loud. We feel a sense of belonging to ourselves and others when we express ourselves clearly, feel understood, and see that other people resonate with our experience in a way that illuminates their own.

We write for fifteen minutes, and some kids ask, "What should I write?" "Well, what was alive for you out there?" I say. "What did you experience?" One girl offers shyly, "The clouds? The color of the sky? The gentle drips of rain on my skin? Is this right?"

"Yes," I say. "If that's what you experienced and it's meaningful to you, then, yes, it's right. Start there. Write it down. What did it make you feel? See if you can either flesh out the feelings and images, by giving them detail and painting a picture with your words, or boil them down to the bones, choosing only the most important nuggets."

"Okay!" she responds enthusiastically. And I know she's learning to trust herself. I know she's learning that what she feels and thinks matters. She tells me she was having a bad day. Things are stressful at home and at school. She doesn't feel like she fits in or belongs anywhere. But after she wrote her poem today, she said she felt better. She said it felt good to connect with her feelings, to write something in her own words, and to create something that was hers.

In my work teaching poetry writing to teens and adults, I have the honor of journeying with my students as they use writing to navigate their way out of numbness and pain and back into life. Every day, I work with people who struggle with figuring out who they are and what matters to them. Some of the kids I work with have deeper issues such as depression, addiction, health and body image issues, learning challenges, trauma, delinquency, gender and sexual identity issues, home and family problems. All of them find healing and empowerment in writing poems. Writing poems helps people believe in themselves. It gives them a way to access and work with their feelings rather than running and hiding from what is painful. Writing poems gives people a real-life experience of their own power and wisdom, and this gives them hope.

I am teaching in Juvenile Hall one day, and a kid asks, "Why should I write a poem? I'm stuck in here. It doesn't matter what I think. My life is not my own." I suggest that their feelings, thoughts, and imaginations are the places where they have the power and freedom to make their own choices, and that they can use that freedom to explore who they are and what matters to them. We begin by writing personifications of the elements, and one kid chooses fire. His poem is fierce and angry. He becomes the flames and burns down the house he grew up in. When he reads his piece, his voice sears the room. Everyone cheers. He smiles for the first time. He tells me that if he can burn his past in a poem, perhaps he can move forward in his life.

I always have students read their pieces in class. Some are so quiet we have to lean forward to hear them, some read with dramatic flair, and some just kick it easy like they're talking to their best friend or singing their favorite song. We clap after each piece because we know the courage and vulnerability it takes to share your poem out loud. I reflect their juiciest lines back to them so they know they've been heard and celebrated, and so the other kids learn what kind of wording and imagery brings a poem to life.

The whole class becomes a learning community, and in hearing their classmates' poems, they realize they're not alone. By the end of class, they've relaxed, their eyes are shining, and I know they've found a path in poetry writing, as I have.

The bell rings, and no one moves. They all look at me like they don't want to leave, like they don't want to lose this. This is my greatest moment. I believe in them and they feel it, and they begin to believe in themselves.

*Go on*, I say, *this is yours. No one can take this from you. Keep listening inside yourselves. Keep noticing what you feel, what moves and inspires you. Make a list. Write it down. See you next week.*

# • 1 •

# Just Write!

*Another word for creativity is courage.*
— HENRI MATISSE

Just write! Don't worry if what you're writing is good or not. Don't worry about whether what you're writing is poetry or not. Don't give any thought to whether it sounds like poetry you've heard or read before. Just write! Trust your gut and just write.

Don't write for anyone else. Write for *you*. Write about what you know. Write about what hurts and write about what you love. Write about what is happening right now in your present experience. Sometimes you're so exhausted you can't move; you're on the underbelly of your wave. That's okay. Be exactly where you are. Write it. Other times you have so much energy you feel like you can fly. Great, go fly, and then come back and write it. Whatever you are experiencing, no matter how awful or wonderful, it is exactly where you need to be to learn who you are and what you're capable of. The way out is through. Writing will help you track your journey through.

When I took classes with the late, great Beat poet Allen Ginsburg, in 1996 at Naropa University in Boulder, Colorado, he always said, "First thought, best thought." This is how he described a spontaneous and fearless way of writing, a way of telling the truth that arises from authentic experience. Pay attention to what you see, hear, and feel, right here, right now. Say yes to whatever ideas and feelings bubble up in you. These are the gifts. Write everything down. Later you can get rid of things you don't like or need. Don't worry about form. Experiment with it. Write to the rhythm of your breath. Make up your own form. Just write!

Dig deep into the caverns of your memories, thoughts, feelings, and experiences. Dig up all the delicious juicy ones, the bubbling-lava angry ones, the lonely miserable ones, the broken self-demeaning ones, the dark secretive ones; dig in, because this is where your poetry lives. When you touch this place in your writing, you will feel it; it's like a combination of fear and salvation. Stay with it.

As for your judge, your inner critic, and any other monsters who feed on your joy and confidence: Tell them to get lost. Tell them you're not afraid of them. Or better yet, invite them to tea! Ask if they'd like to be your friend. Ask what they've got against you, and what they gain by keeping you down. Ask them if they have any helpful information for you. And if not, lock them up at the bottom of the ocean, on the dark side of the moon, in another galaxy, anywhere they can't get to you. Throw away the key. And then, just write.

## What Is a Poem?

*Poetry is thoughts that breathe and words that burn.*
— THOMAS GRAY, "The Progress of Poesy"

A poem is a record of your thoughts and feelings, perceptions and insights. A poem is a photo made with words. If I were a photographer, I would take pictures of the important moments in my life, but as a writer, I use words to capture and express a moment. Yes, I have written poems about beautiful moments, but I began writing poetry to help me through depression and loss and to search for my identity and values. One of the most powerful things about writing is that often we start out feeling hurt or angry, lost or confused, and as we write, we find ourselves on a journey. In naming and describing our feelings, especially the overwhelming ones, we write our way out of the chaos and into clarity. Each piece of writing becomes a map of our journey into and through the maze of our thoughts, feelings, and identity. Writing teaches us to trust ourselves, to stay connected with ourselves through challenging experiences, to write our way through inner storms, and to come out the other side clearer and stronger.

## Poetry Toolbox

A handful of tools will help you bring your poems to life. In the next few pages I offer suggestions on how to find your writing voice, how to use imagery to paint a picture with your words, how to construct metaphor and simile, the hammer and nails of your poetry, which combine unrelated concepts to communicate volumes in just a few words. If metaphor and simile are your hammer and nails, then detail is your glue. The more detail you use, the more tangible your writing becomes. You can try your hand at editing and revising your poems. Some poems you'll want to flesh out with details, while others you may choose to whittle down to their essence, boiling them down to the bones. Experiment with page layout and line breaks to create the visual tone and reading rhythm of your poem. You can have fun choosing which point of view to write from. Different topics warrant writing from different points of view to communicate a certain perspective and make a poem more potent. Let's take a deeper look at each of these tools.

## Writing Voice

Your own voice is the one you want. Trust me, you don't want to sound like anyone else, or you'll never be fulfilled in your writing and it will never become your refuge. If you don't know where or how to find your writing voice, talk to yourself out loud or record yourself speaking, and then do your best to capture your unique speaking style in your writing. Your own way of saying things is the voice you want to write with. If you have a few voices, try writing different poems using different voices. You might surprise yourself and find that when you start writing, a new voice comes through, one that is able to say things you didn't know how to say before. Stay curious. You'll know when you've found your voice, because you won't be able to stop writing: a floodgate will open in you, you'll feel as if you're plugged into an electrical outlet, time will slow down, everything you need will be there, words will come like liquid and lightning, and you will feel deeply, wildly alive.

## *Imagery*

We use imagery in poetry to paint a picture with words that captures what we want to communicate. With imagery we show rather than tell. For example, I can tell you my friend is happy today. Or I can say her eyes are sparkling, there is a song in her voice and a skip in her step. These words make pictures that show you rather than tell you that she is happy.

## *Metaphor and Simile*

As poets we use metaphor and simile to communicate what could be volumes of information in just a few words. Metaphor and simile are the hammer and nails of a poem; they are the tools that build meaning. Metaphor and simile bring together at least two unrelated concepts to identify with or compare to. Metaphor identifies; simile compares. With metaphor we say something *is* something else. She is the sun. He is the ocean. With simile, we use *like* or *as* to compare. She is *like* the sun. Or she is *as* bright *as* the sun. He is *like* the ocean. He is *as* deep *as* the ocean. You know a lot about someone who is as bright as the sun or as deep as the ocean without needing any more spelled out for you.

**Metaphors:** My heart is a garden, my heart is a river, my heart is a sunflower, my heart is a hummingbird, my heart is a locked door. Write your own.

**Similes:** My heart is like a rainstorm, my heart is like a song, my heart is like a lioness, my heart is as tight as a cage, my heart is as smooth as stone. Write your own.

### Flesh It Out or Boil It Down

We usually do two things in poetry. We either flesh it out or boil it down. Poems crave detail. Fleshing it out means giving it all the unique and memorable detail you can dig up. Detail brings a poem to life. For example, I can tell you:

Today, I had lunch under a tree,
and my friend walked by.

Well, you might say, that's nice, but who cares? But if I include specific detail, look what happens:

Today at 12:45 p.m.
I was having lunch
under the big maple tree
on the corner of Stone Street and Stewart Avenue
I was eating a tuna fish sandwich
with pickle relish and too much mayo
on toasted seven-grain bread,
when my friend Johnny walked by
carrying an old LP under his arm.
I kind of have a crush on Johnny.
As he walked by,
he smiled at me
just slightly

out of the corner
of his mouth.

The difference is in the detail, making an unremarkable event memorable. But I can also boil the story down to its bare bones:

Today
I was eating lunch
under a tree,
and Johnny walked by.
He smiled
at me.

Here we have only the most important points of this moment. The sparseness of the piece is evocative. We're told just enough to imagine the feelings that arise when Johnny walks by and smiles. Try fleshing out some of your poems with specifics and detail and boiling others down to the bones.

### Point of View: First, Second, and Third Person

It's fun to write from different points of view. First person is the *I/we* perspective. Second person is the *you* perspective. Third person is the *he/she/it/they* perspective. Try them all, and find what works best for you. Different writing invitations may call forth different points of view, depending on the topic and the angle you want to communicate. Allow yourself to explore and experiment.

Perhaps you find it's easiest to write in first person, from your own perspective, as if you're sharing your own experience:

I hiked up the hill today
and when I got to the top,
I saw a snake slither through the grass.

Or you can write in second person, as if you were writing to or about someone else, inviting the reader to imagine they are having the experience:

You hiked up the hill today
and when you got to the top,
you saw a snake slither through the grass.

Or in third person, writing about someone else, you can create interest in another person, more distance and objectivity, and perhaps suspense:

She hiked up the hill today
and when she got to the top,
she saw a snake slither through the grass.

Choose whatever you like. Try them all!

### Editing and Revising

This book is about helping you get your writing flowing and building a relationship with your writing, and not about editing per se. But I do want to share a couple of ideas about editing and revising. Many people don't enjoy editing and revising, while others find it gratifying, like solving a puzzle or composing a song. I edit my poems hundreds and hundreds of times before I ever think of submitting them for publishing. If you're interested in editing and revising, think in terms of fleshing out your work or boiling it down. Consider adding detail and specifics to enliven a poem and make it unique and memorable. Or make it lean by boiling it down to the bones so only the essential nuggets remain. Work with imagery to show rather than tell. Experiment with metaphor and simile to find the combined concepts that communicate volumes in just a few words. Play with punctuation. Punctuate certain poems, and don't punctuate others. Read your poem out loud to yourself, listening for the rhythm, musicality, and melody. Where do the pauses go? Where do you stop for breath? When you get the lines and flow exactly right, it might sound crazy, but it's as if something in the universe rings. You'll know it when you feel it.

### Page Layout

How you place your poem on the page creates the visual tone and tells people how to read your poem. For example, where does a line break go? A line break is simply where you end one line and move down to the next line. Where you pause and where you take a breath in the rhythm of your poem is usually where your line breaks go. Where one idea stops and another starts is usually a good place for a line break or a new stanza. The beauty of poetry is that you have total freedom to explore and experiment creatively. Write in short, tight phrases down the page or divide your poem into stanzas, forming paragraphs down the page. Choose a specific number of lines for each stanza and repeat this pattern throughout your poem. End some lines in the middle of a phrase or sentence to create a line break that entices your reader to keep going to find out what happens next. How about one word per line? How about centering your poem? Read other people's poetry, and when you find a form you like, copy it. Some people like to use different colors and fonts. I find this hard to read, but if it makes you happy, go wild! Make up your own form and page layout. I've written poems in which I sing a line or two here and there. Do something original. Make it yours.

## How to Use This Book

I'm going to ask you to do something crazy: I'd like you to put away your phone, iPad, and computer for now and do all the writing invitations in this book using old-fashioned paper and pen. I know, crazy, right?! But something magical happens when we put pen to paper. There's something organic in the pressure required to slide ink across paper that engages and stimulates connection between our brain and body. It creates a somatic feedback loop between our hand writing, our brain thinking, and our emotions feeling. Please, at least try it. Discover the connection and fulfillment that come from writing with paper and pen.

I have created and organized the chapters and writing invitations in this book for you to follow like a map on your own journey of exploration, expression, and empowerment. Each invitation will help build and deepen your self-knowledge and self-confidence. There is a desirable order to the progression of chapters and invitations; however, if you prefer to open the book, like cutting a tarot deck, and start wherever you land, please feel free. You can do these writings by yourself, with a friend, or in a group. Why not invite a few friends to join you in a writing group? Meet once a week or once a month. If you don't have a group of friends or peers with whom to write, and if you'd like to meet and write with other poets from all over the country, contact me through my website to join one of my Zoom workshops, at www.meredithheller.com. I'd love to meet you and write with you!

## Writing Journal

Keeping a writing journal is a gift to yourself. Your journal is a place where you can tell yourself the truth, map your journey, and keep track of the beauty that pours out of you. It becomes a friend and companion that can help you:

- listen to yourself
- get clear about what you feel and think
- express what you might otherwise hold inside
- ask for what you want and need
- find understanding, compassion, strength, and peace

If you're like me, you will guard your journal with your life. As you build a writing relationship with yourself, your journal will become one of your most valuable possessions. There was a time in my life when I lugged around a box of about eighty journals — twenty years' worth. They were the record of an extremely challenging era of my life, and I couldn't bear to read back through them, but I couldn't let go of them either. One day a few years ago, in early spring, I woke up and knew I was ready. I pulled out the box, sat on the floor for about ten hours, and read through every journal.

As I read, I began to see cycles of challenge and growth, loss and hope, emotional death and rebirth. I tracked my wounds and my resiliency. There was so much in my past I wanted to push away, but in reading my old journals, I was able to integrate all the experiences and reclaim the lost and neglected parts of myself. I developed a new compassion for myself and respect for what I had endured and how I'd grown. When I finished reading all the journals, I sat on the floor with tears and snot running down my face, pages scattered all over the floor that I ripped out to save and develop later, and I thanked myself for writing during the many years of struggling to find myself. Then I took the journals to the dump.

Afterward, I felt cleansed, as if I'd shed a heavy skin I'd been carrying around with me for a very long time. Reading those journals helped me make peace with my past in a way I couldn't have without revisiting who I'd been and appreciating how I'd grown.

Get yourself a writing journal that appeals to you. It doesn't have to be fancy. Some people like a bound book, while others prefer a spiral-bound notebook. Some people like clean white pages, others prefer lined. A plain old notebook will do just fine. My favorite is a spiral sketchbook that opens flat. I prefer unlined paper so I can write as big or as small as I like, wherever and however I want. Unlined pages allow me to doodle borders around a poem or try my hand at calligraphy. Choose your favorite pen or pencil. My choice is a fine-point felt-tip, nothing I have to push too hard on to get the ink flowing. There is a relationship between you, your pen, and the paper. Feel into this relationship. It will create muscle memory. It will become a ritual that will call you back again and again as a way to access your thoughts and feelings. Soon you will look forward to opening your journal, putting your pen to paper, and entering the mysterious process of summoning the poems that live inside you.

## When and Where to Write

Write before you go to sleep. Write first thing in the morning. Write while you're eating lunch or during a break at work or school. Write when you're sad, depressed, angry, lost, confused, afraid, hopeless, or bored; write when you're full of excitement, joy, anticipation, inspiration, love, longing, accomplishment, or gratitude. Write instead of watching TV, playing video games, trolling social media, texting, or overeating. Make a writing date with yourself. Sit in your favorite chair or curl up in bed. Find a spot outside, allowing nature to find its way into your poem: the rain, the birdsong, the falling leaves. Some people, like me, need absolute quiet to write, while others thrive on stimulation. Try writing alone, in nature, or surrounded by people and noise in a coffee shop, on the subway, at the airport, anywhere you feel inspired. Explore and experiment to find your preferred times and places to write. Trust your own rhythms.

## Writing Sanctuary

If possible, create a special space in your home where you can write — a she shed, a man cave, a writing nook, a creative cove — any space where you won't be distracted and where you can hear your own voice. Make it comfy and cozy, by a window, perhaps. Decorate in Zen-minimalist style, or bring in all the decor that inspires you. If you don't have an actual space for this in your home or your bedroom, create an inner sanctuary. Close your eyes, take a few breaths, and imagine the most inviting space to sit or curl up with your journal and write. Where are you? What does it look like? It's imaginary, so create whatever you want! It can be a real place you've been or a fantasy place. How about the top of a mountain or another planet? Some of my inner sanctuaries include my favorite nook at the Yuba River, a private beach in Big Sur, the treehouse I lived in on the Big Island of Hawaii. Once you've created your inner sanctuary, you can write anywhere. Let's get started.

# Who Am I?

*I am large. I contain multitudes.*
— WALT WHITMAN, "Song of Myself"

Who am I? This is a deep question. We can answer it using all the ways we normally identify ourselves, our work, our studies, our interests, our relationships. Or we can dig deeper. Too early in life we are asked to narrow ourselves in order to fit in. As children, we're curious about everything, and we instinctively follow what gives us joy and fulfillment. But as we grow up, we are asked to fit ourselves into small and specific containers of who we are and what we do. We are so much more than we usually allow ourselves.

Yes, we are children, siblings, students, parents, partners, friends, workers, seekers, athletes, poets, artists, musicians, and a hundred other words that help define, categorize, distinguish, and connect us. But we are also part of everything and everyone we love, all our experiences, all the lessons that hurt us and grow us, and everything that moves us.

INVITATION: Consider all the beautiful, challenging, wild, and humbling things and experiences that express who you are. Find as many ways as you can to identify and define yourself. Be willing to expand how you know yourself. Start close to home, the solid things you know about who you are, and then branch out and take some chances. Surprise yourself!

 JUST WRITE! Answer the question, Who am I? by starting with the phrase *I am...* and writing a poem in the form of a list. This can be done as a solo writing invitation, as a dyad with another person, or in a group. If you're doing this with one or more people, have one person ask another, "Who are you?" The other person will answer, "I am..." Whatever the person answers, the questioner simply says, "Thank you" and repeats the question, "Who are you?" Change roles after a few minutes. If you say or hear something you like, make a quick note of it. Usually people start with the basics: I am a girl or a woman. I am a boy or a man. I am a teenager. I am an artist, a dancer, an athlete. I am a math person or a literature person. I am an introvert or an extrovert. By the end of the exercise, people are breaking out creatively. I have heard: I am the wind, I am a thunderstorm, I am the earth, I am midnight, I am a swarm of bees, I am a juicy mango, I am a sign that says "Hello!"

### Examples

*Who Am I? — Chris, 17*

I am the air and the sky
and a blue so clean you can drink it

I am the teeth of the earth
that turn everything back into compost

I am the smell of decaying leaves
in the woods where the mushrooms grow

I am the silence before the storm
and the boom of lightning when it strikes

I am the empty street at night
listening to the wind

I am my mother and my father
yelling and not hearing each other

I am the dark freedom
right before I fall asleep

I am the song you hear in your head
but can never remember well enough to sing

I am the stars in Orion's belt
and the spurs on his boots

I am the starfish
regenerating an arm

I am the tears that make up the ocean
that salty mouth that ate my brother's boat.

*I Am — Eve, 9*

I am a tiny speck of hope in the wind.
I am the one that wakes you up with my song.
I am the one whose heart is pounding
before a performance,
I am excited, I am excited, I am excited.
I am the gentle whistle of the wind.
I am the instrument that moves with the day.
I am the one who can't be seen but can be heard.
I am the thing that whirls and runs
because of a ball of music inside you.

## Breaking Open

*You have to keep breaking your heart until it opens.*

— RUMI

Sometimes it's hard to get started in our writing. Often we have so many overwhelming, conflicting, and confusing thoughts and feelings that we get blocked and cannot access any of them. When this happens, it's helpful to have a reserve of questions to ask ourselves, questions that help us break the ice and break open, so we can get to the core of what we're feeling and find the words to name these feelings. Naming our feelings makes it easier to sort them out. Naming gives us the power to work with what's there.

 INVITATION: Read through the Breaking-Open Statements below, and choose a few that provide an entry point into what you're feeling in this moment or into something you'd like to explore in your writing.

 JUST WRITE! Complete one or more of the Breaking-Open Statements below. Read back through what you've written, and choose your best lines, words, and images. Use these to write a poem expressing how you feel, what you're going through, what you're learning about yourself.

### · Breaking-Open Statements ·

If I could say what I really mean, I would say...
My heart longs for...
My body wants...
What I most desire is...
I'm sad because...
I made a mistake when I...
It really pisses me off when...
I'm angry at this person because...
When I'm anxious, I...
I feel stuck when...
What really stresses me out is...
I feel hopeless when...
How I work with illness, disability, or a current
        challenge is...
To calm my anxiety, I...
I am proud of myself for...
My wisdom says...
If I open my heart...
I feel inspired when...
I feel most alive when...
My happy place is...

## Example

*My Illness Isn't Beautiful — Katie, 19*

My illness isn't beautiful
I do not bleed roses
The tears that I cry
Are not drops from the ocean
My illness is not beautiful

My illness is in my stomach
Could eat every cookie in the kitchen
And still feel empty
Forever hungry,
But for what?

My illness is in my legs
Like cannonballs; I trudge
Tons tied to my ankles
As I walk through the hall
But alas, they never see

My illness is in my throat
Filled to the brim with boiling water
Gasping for air
Choking on words
And they wonder why I stopped raising my hand

It's "Happiness is a choice!"
And "You're too fortunate for this!"
As if I don't wish on every eyelash

For a glimpse of the sunlight
That you see

It's the walls
The walls
The walls
I reach out my hand
But they're not windows after all

They've left me in a box
Where it's cold and dark
So even with my best friends
It's just me
And my walls

Now here I shiver
At the foot of my bed
My eyes black holes
I'm an empty shell
With shoulders, knees, and toes

So once all my dreams
Have been sipped out by a straw
Can you finally see that
My illness isn't as beautiful
As you might have thought?

But now here I stand
With color in my cheeks
I've fought for so long

To feel anything at all
My glow when I see loved ones

I cry tears of joy at the movies
I sing songs of strength
Lyrics surge through my bones
I can move mountains now
Pride fills my insides

But please, do not forget
It's my progress that is beautiful
My illness is not.

### • Dig Deeper •

What gives you energy?

What drains you?

How do you nurture yourself?

Who or what helps you feel safe and protected?

Who do you go to when you need help, support,
    guidance?

Who or what most inspires you, and why?

What ways do you use to numb or distract yourself
    from what you're feeling?

What are your strengths and weaknesses?

Who are your closest friends, family, allies, and why?

What do you love most about your friends and family?

How do you define health?

If you could travel anywhere in the world, where would
    you go, and why?

If you won the lottery, what would you do with the
money?

Which humanitarian or environmental cause would
you like to support, and why?

## Childhood Photo

Look at a photo of yourself when you were a young child, three
to five years old. It's hard to believe you were ever that small
or young. While we grow and change throughout our lives,
something in the eyes remains constant. When we look at a
photo of ourselves and into our eyes, sometimes we can see
ourselves looking back. What does this feel like? What can we
learn from our childhood self? Does your younger self have
a message for you? Or do you have some wisdom for them?

 INVITATION: Choose a photo of yourself from when
you were about three to five years old. Pick one
where you're looking into the camera. Spend some
time gazing into your own eyes until you see the person you
know as yourself looking back. Say hello.

 JUST WRITE! Ask your younger self if they have a
message for you. Write down anything that comes
to your mind. Trust anything you hear. Do you rec-
ognize yourself? What did you know about yourself at this
age? What has remained true for you? What has changed?
Did you become who you thought you would? You can try
this with photos of yourself at a variety of ages and see what
messages and insights your younger self has for you.

## Examples

### *At Six and Sixteen — Ellie, 16*

You and I
we're not so different
the tilt of your head
the sadness in your eyes
your lips pressed tight

You're standing still for the camera
but I know inside you're really dancing
I see that little cowlick in your hair
I see the wind blowing through your body
like music only you can hear

Let's make a pinkie-promise
no matter how angry we get
no matter how much our heart breaks
promise we'll always dance

### *Child of Hope — Raney, 12*

Child of green
Child of blue
Child of lush and wild
Child who runs and laughs and plays
While her planet and friend always smile

Child of rhythm, child of pace
Child of clear and deep

Child whose feet thump and bound
Like a heart stirring in sleep

Child of legacies, child of hope
Child of a world now divided
Child who together with other survivors
Will form to wake the misguided

## Born with Instructions

*It takes courage to grow up and become who you really are.*
— E. E. CUMMINGS AS QUOTED IN MATTHEW BURGESS,
*Enormous Smallness: A Story of E. E. Cummings*

While our parents tried to do their best, most likely there are things you wish they'd done differently. Imagine that when you were born, your parents received a one-page letter of instructions specifically about you. This letter informs your parents about the kind of person you want to be and about how you'd like them to nurture and raise you so you can grow into the person you came here to be, the best version of yourself you can imagine.

 INVITATION: Think about all the ways you wish you had been raised and nurtured. What would you have told your parents about who you are if you'd had the chance when you were born? What should they know about you so that they could raise you to become the person you want to be?

**JUST WRITE!** Write a poetic list of instructions for your parents or caretakers, telling them exactly what to do to help you become the person you want to be. (Bonus: When you're done, you'll have a list of things you can do to help nurture yourself to become the person you know you are!)

## Example

*Nature Child — Kelly, 15*

Make sure to take me out in nature every day so I am
     connected to the earth and sky.
Take me to rivers and oceans and let me play in the water so
     I grow brave and curious.
Teach me how to build treehouses so I always have my own
     special place to go.
Plant a vegetable garden every year so I learn about seeds
     and plants and the cycles of life and death.
Teach me how to cook so I can always feed myself and others.
Let me sleep under the stars so I feel connected to the
     universe.
Get me a puppy so I learn how to love and care for
     something and so I have a companion.
Teach me to speak at least two other languages so I can talk
     to more people and travel.
Laugh at dinnertime so that eating together becomes
     something I look forward to.
Go for walks every night so I am not afraid of the dark.
Let me sleep late on the weekend because my best dreams
     happen in the morning.

Teach me the importance of exercise to keep my body
    strong and flexible.

Give me lots of hugs and encouragement so I feel loved.

Teach me healthy boundaries so I learn to respect and value
    myself and others.

Guide me to study and learn the things that excite me so I
    can make a life and find work that I love.

## Self-Portrait

*I am my own experiment. I am my own work of art.*
— MADONNA

This invitation requires more than just looking at ourselves
in the mirror and writing about what we see. This is about
describing who we are, inside and out, with the kind of words
that convey insight into our relationships with ourselves. We
often focus on what we don't like about ourselves: we're too
skinny, too fat; we're good at this but not so good at that;
we wish we were better at math or more artistic. The media
makes it impossible, if you're a girl, to feel like you fit in and
are desirable, unless you're thin, gorgeous, and feminine.
Likewise, boys and men must be athletic, handsome, and
successful. But if we could learn to see ourselves with eyes
of acceptance for all our beautiful and imperfect humanness,
we would treat ourselves and others with greater kindness.

 INVITATION: Write a poetic self-portrait, like painting
a picture of yourself with words. How do you see
yourself? What do you know about yourself?

**JUST WRITE!** Look at yourself in the mirror. Just notice. Don't judge. Just accept and say hello. Write a list of what you see: long legs, tan skin, strong belly, big feet, wild hair. Next, write a list of all the adjectives you can use to describe yourself: *kind*, *wise*, *silly*, *creative*, *fierce*, *loving*, *loyal*, *truthful*. Now take your lists and choose a few points from each, and write about yourself as if you were painting a picture with words to tell someone who you are. Describe aspects of your appearance, and weave in your interests, accomplishments, fears, dreams. You, like all of us, are a work in progress. Be kind and patient with yourself. It takes a lifetime to become who we want to be.

## Examples

### *Queen of the Gorgons — Amelia, 15*

Eyes of tinted glass
behind oval frames
turn the world
a shade of blue.
I sit before my mirrors
casting out my demons
my body a vessel
of cracked clay.
Half-moon smile on my lips
beaded serpents around my neck
hissing and cursing
at a world that curses me back.

*Not Quite Ripe — Katie, 19*

I am not quite ripe yet
I was born on the feeble branch
of the lemon tree
I smell like a clean home
I have ridges like fingerprints
unique to me alone.

I am not quite ripe yet
green blends into yellow
like watercolor paint
kissing on a canvas
or like clashing currents
in an angry sea.

I am not quite ripe yet
I exist in a space between
child and adult
possibility and stagnation
reaching for better
and content with the present.

I am not quite ripe yet,
and maybe that's okay.

## My Name

There are tribes of aboriginal people in Africa whose members, when they're very young, go off into the wild, alone, to learn their birth song. When they know their song they return to the tribe and teach it to everyone, and this becomes their name. The tribe sings their name song to them their whole life as a way of identifying and honoring them. Even when they are dying, the tribe sings their song to them so they will remember who they are as they travel into the next world. Our names are how we identify ourselves. They are the affirmations of who we are; they are what we answer yes to when someone calls. Our parents choose our names. Some names are handed down from a grandparent or family friend. Some people change their names to one they feel better suits them. Our names are a song of pitch and rhythm, syllable and tone. They set the mood for how we identify ourselves.

 **INVITATION:** Think about your name. Do you know the story of how and why your parents chose it? Have you ever asked them? Were you named after someone? If so, who? What is the meaning of your name? What is the sound, rhythm, tone, and feel of your name? Is it sharp or round, smooth or bumpy? Does it end in an *ahh* sound or a clipped consonant? Does your name have double letters? Is it a palindrome? Do you feel your name fits you? What powers does your name give you? Would you change your name if you could? If so, what name would you choose, and why?

 **JUST WRITE!** Write about your name. Say it out loud to yourself a few times. Listen to the sound, tone, rhythm, and shape of the word. Turn it over in your mouth and taste it. What images and feelings come to you when you consider your name? What does your name mean to you? Does your name come with a story? Do you like your name? Would you change it if you could? Do something creative with the letters of your name, especially unusual letters like *z* or *x*. Try turning these letters into an animal or an instrument; make it dance, fight, sing, bloom.

## Example

*Ava Gloria — Ava, 14*

Ava Gloria sounds solemn, sacred; the sound of holy words, recited and resounded. A prayer of brilliance, golden glory, a prayer for cardinal wings to fly away with. A name befitted of a lion queen, ready to stand like a statue and be adored. Sounds like a speech belonging to a saint, uttered and hushed, while white votive candles look on silently to the pews.

As much as Ava belongs to the little bird my mother saw in the snow that day, small, sturdy, and red from pecking, beak to perky tail feathers, Gloria belongs to my grandmother; Nana, I called her, when I was only small and soft.

The child of two immigrants from Mexico. The youngest of enough sisters she could get lost in them. Gloria slid into the middle of her name too, right between Carmen and Masón. When marriage swallowed up the Masón, and her sisters grew older each day, she clung to Catholicism. Little prayers and idols of Guadalupe gave my mother her own in-between name, strung up on her cabinets.

Ava Gloria fits me like Carmen's hand-me-downs, dusty and sweet, and a little loose on me, lived in by someone whose story I only know the edges of. I will wrap myself in these stories, take pieces for myself, keep them even once they are worn down and torn up, and no longer beautiful, until they fit me, stitched into my soul in gilded gold that looks, almost, holy.

# · 3 ·

# Stone Soup

*To be nobody-but-yourself — in a world which is doing its best, night and day, to make you everybody else — means to fight the hardest battle which any human being can fight.*

— E. E. CUMMINGS, *A Miscellany (Revised)*

We are made, tuned, and tempered by everything we love and everything we struggle with. Every experience, every relationship, everyone we come into contact with, everything we fight or embrace, makes us who we are. Here is a chance to write an empowering list of things you are made of, things that describe you, things that make you shine. You can refer to this list when you want to remember what makes you, you.

 INVITATION: Think about all the things that make you who you are and describe what's unique about you. Think of things that contain elements of what you value and what gives meaning to your life. Think about your favorite things, food, people, and activities. Make this a list that empowers you or gives you a deeper sense of yourself and your purpose.

**JUST WRITE!** Write a list of all the things you love: people, activities, music, social causes, food, clothing. Include everything you've been learning about yourself through your writing. Allow certain things to be funny, sad, deep. This is part of what makes you unique. Choose things that help you feel good about yourself. Celebrate yourself in this poem. Try starting with one of these phrases: *I am made of, I am from*, or *Where I'm from*, and repeat this phrase throughout your poem as you like.

## Examples

### *I Am Made Of — Candice, 17*

I am made of hopscotch
and coffee ice cream
a map of the Serengeti
a love song in A-minor
I am made of a scar on my left eyebrow from a dog bite
unforgivable things said out loud
fear of rejection
salsa on blue corn chips
I am made of bitten fingernails
an archipelago of sadness
a bowl of fresh-picked arugula
homemade soup
I am made of a breakable heart
shallow breath
a conclusive NO
a trembling YES
one pair of doe-colored sneakers dappled with rain

### *Where I'm From — Katie, 19*

I'm from the cherry blossom tree exploding in April
And the dilapidated treehouse behind the looming trees
I'm from a blue fighter fish named Davey and two small
    aquatic frogs
I'm from fairy houses next to the track at my school

I'm from cargo shorts and foursquare
And always getting hit in the head with a basketball
I'm from Luna Lovegood and Neville Longbottom
Always looking for the best in others
but not seeing it in themselves

I'm from Crash Course History
and store-bought cinnamon rolls on Friday nights
Anything to fill the deafening emptiness

Now I'm from Jack White blaring in my earphones
as I strut down Sixth Avenue
I'm from small apartments crammed full of friends
I'm from drag shows on Fridays
and fighting for the climate on Saturdays

I'm from dollar pizza at 2 a.m.
And "text me when you're home safe"
I'm from dark yoga studios with loud music
Washing my sweat off in the shower
like shedding a shell of my old self

I'm from crying enough to fill swimming pools
And laughing until my bones crack
I'm from my mom always telling me:
>  All will be well
>  All will be well.

## My Mask

*Man is least himself when he talks in his own person.*
*Give him a mask, and he will tell you the truth.*
— OSCAR WILDE, *Intentions*

We all have a mask, or a few masks, we wear. Masks are good. They're useful. We need them. They're like the different hats or uniforms we put on for different events when different skill sets are required of us. Having a few masks in your toolbox or your makeup bag is a good thing. Like performers and dancers who wear a mask to bring a character to life or create a caricature of a feeling, we wear masks to bring out different qualities at different moments. Masks can hide or protect certain aspects of us while highlighting and revealing others. They can help us uncover and discover hidden parts of ourselves. The trick is knowing which mask you're wearing and why, and being able to take your mask off and knowing, or at least questioning, who or what is underneath the mask when you take it off. I have a friend, Rachel, who is a mask maker. She takes a mold of her own face and then adds clay, paint, fur, feathers, and antlers to build fantastical masks of creatures, animals, goblins, gargoyles, and goddesses. She says the most important question is, *Are we more or less of ourselves when we wear a mask?* What are some of the masks you wear? Do they hide or reveal your true self? Who or what is under your mask when you take it off?

 INVITATION: Think about all the different masks you wear. Perhaps there is one you wear at school, one for work, another when you're with your family, and yet another one you put on with your friends. Let's consider that these masks are allies and that they have important information for us. What are the qualities of the masks you wear? Why do you wear them, and what do they do for you? What aspects of you do they hide, and what aspects do they reveal? Who or what is under the mask when you take it off?

 JUST WRITE! Choose and describe one of your masks. What does it look like? What are you able to do or be when you wear it? Where did it come from? Did you learn it from someone, or did you invent it yourself? Does it serve you or hinder you? What does it hide about you? What does it reveal? What are the attributes of this mask, positive and negative? Are you aware when you have it on? Are you able to take it off? Who or what is under the mask when you remove it?

## Example

*My Smile — Kevin, 16*

My smile is a mask I wear.
Underneath
I am sad and bare.

My cool exterior hides
the angry animal
who lives inside.

I wish I could show you
my true face.
You would not like the taste.

I tried to take it off last night
but even I was scared
it would bite.

What I really want to say
Is, I'm sorry for that day.
How long do I have to pay?

I cannot look myself in the eye.
Without my mask,
I just cry.

## Stone Soup

I'm borrowing from my favorite fairy tale, "Stone Soup." You know the one: A band of hungry travelers are passing through a village empty-handed, except for a cooking pot. The villagers don't want to share their food, so the travelers simply fill their pot with stream water, drop in a big stone, and put it on the fire to heat. The villagers grow curious. *What are you doing?* they ask. *Well,* the travelers say, *we're making stone soup, but it still needs a garnish for flavor.* So one by one, the curious villagers bring a sprig of this and a snippet of that — a carrot, a stalk of celery, an onion, a potato — to add flavor to the stone soup, and by the end of the evening, there's a pot of soup big enough to feed everyone. I just love this! Now connect this idea to the adage that it takes a village to raise a child and that we're going to ask each person in our community for an ingredient of themselves that we can put in our personal "soup pot of self." For example, when I was growing up, if someone didn't like me, I would wonder, *What's wrong with* me? But if someone didn't like my best friend, Michelle, she would say, *What's wrong with* them? I saw that confidence as an ingredient I needed in my own soup. I wanted it, and I set out to learn it for myself. I had another friend, Jennifer, who went to an all-girls Catholic school. She always wore lingerie under her uniform so she had a secret to smile about when the nuns put her down. She told me, *The rules only apply to you if you let them!* I knew I needed this ingredient in my self-soup too. I've also been inspired by a few of my favorite sheroes and heroes from novels who had ingredients I wanted, such as bravery, resourcefulness, and adventurousness. What qualities do you want for your self-soup?

 INVITATION: Think about the people you know in your life and community (or characters from your favorite books or movies), and write a list of the ingredients each of them has that could benefit you.

 JUST WRITE! For each person you've chosen, describe the ingredient they have, why you want it, and how you can use it in your own life.

## Example

*A Pot of People Soup — Max, 14*

Smarts from Auntie Josie,
    Everyone needs smarts
Humor from Grandpa Jack,
    Helps me get through life without taking things so
        seriously
Determination from my brother, Kai
    He really knows how to apply himself and get things
        done
Creativity from my sister, Rosie,
    She can draw and paint and make anything into art
Wisdom from my best friend, Grayson,
    He has a way of knowing what's important in life and
        keeping me straight on
Confidence from my teacher, Mr. Henry,
    He really believes in me and I see how this helps me
        to apply myself and do my best
Love from my mom, Carol,
    I hope to always love my family and friends the way
        my mom loves me
Magic and courage from Harry Potter,
    I admire him. He is so independent and doesn't let
        anything stop him
Curiosity, that's all mine,
    I'm interested in so many things, and I love to ask
        questions and learn new stuff.

## Portrait of a Friend

This is a fun activity to do with a friend. It can bring you closer, make you laugh, reveal some vulnerability, and help you see how someone else views you. Get ready to engage your powers of observation and perception to paint a picture of your friend with poetic words. Writing a portrait of a friend is a gift we can give another person to help them see themselves the way we do, perhaps more clearly and with more kindness. By writing about another person, we also learn more about ourselves.

 INVITATION: Write a poetic portrait of a friend. Use all your powers of perception. Include appearance, interests, your relationship with this person, everything you already know about them, and perhaps some things you've learned just now. Finally, be open to what you might learn about yourself by writing about your friend.

 JUST WRITE! Partner up with a friend and sit facing each other. Take a few moments to simply observe your partner, without judgment; just see what you see. Begin to write as you take in the other person, painting their portrait by describing them with words. Notice what the person looks like. Notice the expression in their eyes. How do they hold their head, their mouth, their shoulder? What do these things tell you about this person? Include all the things you know about them, what they like and dislike, what makes them happy and sad, what makes them tick. Include what you appreciate about this person; even if you don't know them well yet, what is your sense of who they are? Trust what you feel. Now turn your attention around, and notice what the details you've picked out about this person tell you about yourself. When you're finished, thank your friend and share your poetic portrait of them.

## Example

*Portrait of Claire — Loryn, 15*

Tell me, yellow girl
where is it you found will
drunk in the fuzzy dream
of lust and ladybugs
broken maternal reflections

Tell me, simple sweet pea
how is it the colors find you
welcomed by your wheat fingers
I'd think would be tied behind you
in fear of raving

Show me, pale moon
the way to open today
and stomp on the past
Your skin is wet from rebirth
I see the clear her, closer
each time you blink

Teach me, gentle one
not anger but acceptance

how to laugh
as though gulped by the wind

Promise me, mother's dangling star
I'll be you someday
with wooden hair and sky-glass eyes
voice old-soul and fresh purity
hate and pain exhaled away
down from your soaring flight
swinging Virgo
of healing tilted heart.

## Poetic Biography

*Life shrinks or expands in proportion to one's courage.*
— ANAÏS NIN, *The Diary of Anaïs Nin*, vol. 3

At some point in life, we'll have the need or opportunity to write a bio about ourselves, telling others who we are; where we went to school and what we studied; our work experience and hobbies; and all our successes so someone will believe in us and hire us for our dream job. Many bios, while impressive, can be bland and unimaginative. Let's be brave and write poetic bios about ourselves that express who we are, in full color. Include some of the things you're learning about yourself from the poems you've been writing.

 INVITATION: Write your bio in a way that inspires you and expresses your unique self. What if you were writing a bio to find a best friend rather than a job?

What would you say about yourself to let others know who you truly are and what you're made of?

 **JUST WRITE!** Write a fun, poetic, wild, outrageous, colorful, silly, imaginative, vulnerable bio about who you are, how you spend your time, and what matters to you.

## Examples

### Superhero — Greggory, 17

I'm a young man with big dreams. When I look in the mirror, I see the whole world, and like Michael Jackson sang, I wanna MAKE A CHANGE! I'm as bright and ambitious as a Monday morning. I'm like a brass trumpet screaming a yellow song at sunrise. You'll find me trail-running through the San Francisco headlands, stopping only for coyote crossings and to talk to red-tailed hawks. At home, I like to read adventure novels. I'm inspired by heroes who help others. I believe we all have superpowers. Mine is encouraging others to be their best. My dream is to travel the world helping people awaken their superpowers. I rarely take no for an answer.

### Celtic Heart — Meredith

An ancient elfin-child with a Celtic heart. A gypsy-poet philosopher with a penchant for humor and a pocketful of wisdom. A melodic priestess who weaves easily between light and dark, major and minor. A woman who thrives in nature, howls with the wolves, and delights in the wild beauty of life.

# · 4 ·

# Time Capsule

*The past beats inside me like a second heart.*
— John Banville, *The Sea*

We all have a pair of magic glasses that allows us to see into our past. Some people see only the hurtful memories, while others see only the good. Both are valuable. Both provide substantive material for writing and for becoming integrated and whole human beings. Let's put on our magic glasses and take a look!

## I Remember

To remember is to summon the past. Memory is a rich reservoir, a treasure trove for poetic writing. Some memories we push down and try to forget because they're too painful; others we keep reliving. Writing about memories, especially painful ones, helps us become whole again. When we dredge up old memories and sift through the debris, we find the scattered, lost, or abandoned pieces of ourselves, and when we weave ourselves back together with all the good, the bad, the brilliant, the messy, and the miserable parts, we come to greater peace with who we are. Memory offers an abundance of emotionally packed information to write about. The tiniest thing can spark a memory.

 INVITATION: Close your eyes and stir your memories. Be open to whatever pops up to the surface, and grab a memory that really lights up. Is it an old friend, a lover, a pet, a teacher, a grandparent, a place, an injury, an exhilarating or terrible experience? Use your senses to conjure the smells, sights, sounds, and feelings. Let the memory play before your inner eye like a movie.

 JUST WRITE! Start your poem with the phrase *I remember...* or *I remember the time...* See where it takes you. Track the details. What's happening? Where are you? What season or year is it? Who else is there? What are you doing? What are you feeling and thinking? What are you wearing? What are the smells, sights, sounds? What do you feel in your body as you review this memory? Write about the memory as if it's happening now.

## Example

### I Remember — Anahera, 12

I remember that time when the dusty gold smeared across the horizon and the glowing embers of the newborn stars laughed harmony into our souls.

I remember being nervous, my palms sweating, fiddling with my fingers, and you raising your hand, your lilting voice like a thousand singing birds.

I remember you walking toward me, then leaping in gallops like a prancing horse speckled with nutmeg. You, calling my name, followed with yours, sounding like a song on your gifted tongue.

I remember the words I longed to say to you, coming out croaky and stuttering, my *hi!* turning into an inaudible whisper.

We strolled through a wood in blissful shade, darkness enveloping us in silence. I remember you trying to break the silence, asking me what I like to do.

Me, stammering like a toad with hiccups. The time passing too quickly. Me wanting to sit with you for longer. I remember you saying *bye*, and my heart almost breaking.

You were my first friend in this new world. But I healed when you said you'd see me again tomorrow.

I remember the time I met you. I remember the time you said goodbye. I remember the time we became best friends.

## Home

*There's no place like home.*
— DOROTHY, in *The Wizard of Oz*, L. Frank Baum

Home is a place but it's also a feeling. We feel at home in certain places and with certain people. To feel at home is a rare kind of special. It fills our hearts and bodies with a powerful sense of peace and belonging. So what makes somewhere home? Where do you feel at home, and what elements go into making a place a home? For some people, home is where they grew up. For others, home is a place they've created that feels cozy and familiar, where they have everything they need. Still other people have the ability to make themselves at home wherever they are. Are you a homebody, or do you thrive on being out and about, on the move, at home in your own skin?

INVITATION: What makes a place home for you? What makes you feel at home? Think about your childhood home. What do you remember about it? Did you feel at home there? Did it feed your heart and soul? What elements made it feel like home? The feeling of home includes the physical space, the people, and the sounds, smells, foods, sights, conversations, pets. Home is where you feel most, well, at home. Where is this for you?

JUST WRITE! Write about a place that feels like home. Describe the space, people, pets, feelings, memories, smells, foods, sights, sounds, and conversations you remember. What makes it home? You can write about your childhood home, your favorite home, or your current home. If you don't have a place that feels like home, imagine one and explore what it would be like, how you would feel there, what would make it home.

## Examples

*My Old Home — Raney, 11*

Six months ago today, I sadly left my old Ontario home to come here, to Laguna, California. I miss Ontario every day, our old stone house with the creaky front door, the left window in my room that I could never open myself, cold October mornings when my breath would spiral out of my mouth like smoke from Grandpa Jake's pipe, flurries of crunchy leaves that would form piles to jump in, and summers when the hill behind our house danced with shimmering golden-green grass.

My mom always tells me that my face looks like a field of grass. My pale hazel eyes like the grass, the smattering of freckles under my eyes like seeds that drop, the curls of my hair like birds swooping down to collect the seeds, and my long legs always galloping like the breeze of stirred grass. But now, every day I wake up to screaming sea gulls and waves crashing onto prickly sand. I use the birds to pull away, their wings floating my mind up, up, and away.

*I Am from the Home of the Illegals — Alex, 16*

I am from the home of the illegals
from the Spanish ghetto streets
where people vulture like eagles.

Where people run down the block
with their ice-cream carts
trying to sell their products
trying to make a start.

Scrapping cars from the gutter
to scrape up a few dollars.
Buy smoke, buy drugs
for a moment of thunder.

Where the homeless bums
drink until they sleep in the streets.
Where old dudes act like zombies
'cuz they've been high all week.

It's a hectic home
there's drama in the streets
the people stay silent
the people stay mute.

Poverty and robbers
fill our homes and our streets.
Crime stays committed
it shoots us in our sleep.

## Hiding Place

*Poems hide. In the bottoms of our shoes,*
*they are sleeping.... What we have to do*
*is live in a way that lets us find them.*

— NAOMI SHIHAB NYE, "Valentine for Ernest Mann"

Everyone needs a little hiding space all to themselves. Many of us had a secret hiding place when we were kids. Many adults have places like this too. We've heard of man caves and lady coves, and more recently she sheds, bitch barns, and witch wings! Did you have a secret hiding place when you were a kid? I did. I actually had a few. In the summer, I loved to hide out in the bathtub, no water, just the cool porcelain against my skin, my pillow lining the back of the tub, the shower curtain drawn for privacy. I'd spend hours in my tub, reading. I also had my own clubhouse under the big pine tree in the front yard. These were places where I could be alone, hear my own voice, make art, read and write, watch clouds, daydream.

 INVITATION: Think about a hiding place you had as a kid, or one you have now. Where is it? How did you find it? Does anyone else know about it? Why and when do you go there? What do you do there?

 JUST WRITE! Write about your childhood hiding place or a hiding place you have now. Where is it? Is it inside or outside? How big or small is it? What does it smell like? What do you keep in there? How do you feel being there? What do you do there? If you didn't or don't have a hiding place, feel free to invent one.

## Example

*Hiding Place — Matteo, 15*

Quiet
alone
light slanted
through branches
rustle of leaves

songs of birds
rhythm of feet
chants of voices
my own breath
the salty taste of sweat on my lips
a place of floaty dreams
between awake and asleep
comic books
broken crayons and crumpled paper
peanut-butter cookie crumbs
an old baseball cap,
me.

## Family Portraits

*You think you're enlightened,*
*go spend a week with your family!*
— RAM DASS, "The Game of Enlightenment"

Families have healthy relationship dynamics of love, loyalty, and support but also dysfunctional dynamics of secrets, abuse, competition, and things unspoken. In my family there were things we didn't tell my father and things we didn't tell my sister, so of course I wondered what they didn't tell me. This bred in me a sense of mistrust and also a quest to tell the truth. We carry our family patterns around with us and unconsciously replicate them in our own relationships, unless we get clear about what they are and choose to keep the ones we like and change the ones that no longer serve us.

INVITATION: Choose a family photograph. Look at the people in the photo and think about the relationship dynamics of your family. Who are you closest to? Who can you be yourself with? Where is the tension? Are there family secrets? Is there anything that is off limits to talk about? Do you enjoy or dread being with your family, and why?

 JUST WRITE! Looking at your family photo, write about the feelings that arise in you about your family. You can write from your own perspective, or you can try writing from the imagined perspective of one of your family members. Take a clear look at the patterns that play out in your family, good and bad. All families have their issues. What do you appreciate about your family? What drives you crazy? What would you change if you could?

## Example

*The Braid of Existence — Sophie, 10*

The mother, toasted skin and long coal-black hair, has a braid on each side of her head, joining into one. One daughter has green eyes and hair like a chestnut pony. Her skin is like a peach in the sun, spattered with freckles like a paint canvas. The second daughter has cocoa-colored skin and eyes gray like stone. Her hair is tightly curled, falling neatly down her back. The three women's hair is braided into one big braid, and like their hair, their hands too are interwoven.

The women are wrapped in the silver of the clouds. Birds fly around their heads, showing the passing of time. The three women are bound together, connecting the future with the past, braiding them together like their hair.

The mother looks into the future, her back turned on what came before. The first sister watches the past with focused green eyes. The second sister, with cocoa skin, gazes at the present, with eyes like a hawk; she sees what others may not.

The three women represent the past, present, and future, and all are of equal importance to each other. Each is one part of the braid of existence, like a mother and two daughters.

### • Dig Deeper •

Who in your family do you go to for nurturing?

Who do you go to for safety and protection?

Who do you seek out for advice, guidance, wisdom?

Which family member is most significant in your life?

What draws you to them?

What do you appreciate about this person?

What do you find challenging about this person?

What are the best and worst things you share with this person?

What works and doesn't work in this relationship?

What do you learn about yourself from this person?

How have you changed from knowing this person?

What do you wish you could do differently with this person?

Is there anything you'd like to say to this person?

## Time Capsule

A time capsule is a generational scrapbook in which we pull together all the elements that identify and define us, showing who we are and what we value at a certain time in history, leaving a record of what we want to be remembered for by future generations. Let's have some fun and create our own time capsules.

 **INVITATION:** Make a personal time capsule. Think about who you are, what you value, and what you want to be remembered for. Think about what you would want someone in the future to know about you.

 **JUST WRITE!** Imagine you're gathering a pile of the most significant items that represent your values, interests, accomplishments, and goals. Consider areas of study, music, poetry, ideas, books, movies, food, clothing, nature, hobbies, sports, friends, family, and more. Make sure everything you choose is unique and special for you, what you value and love and want to be remembered for. Write about what you put in your time capsule and why. Make it serious, witty, poetic, metaphorical, sentimental. You choose!

### Example

*Time Capsule — Dawn, 12*

My poems
Songbirds
The colors of sunset

Dried lavender petals
Homemade peach ice cream
Blue sea glass
Monarch butterflies
Harry Potter books
Jar of car exhaust
Melting ice caps
Endangered species
Honeybees
Green scarab beetle pin from my grandmother
Handmade purple wool mittens
Sound of my baby brother crying
Vegetable seeds
Pail of ocean water and sand
Full moon
My best friend, Cara, laughing
Needle and thread
My blues harmonica
Chocolate-chip cookies
Ripped jeans
Glitter pens of all colors
A tiny jar of tears

# 5

# Come to Your Senses

*now the ears of my ears awake*
*and now the eyes of my eyes are opened*
— E. E. CUMMINGS, "i thank You God for most this amazing day"

Our five senses — sight, smell, hearing, taste, and touch — are apertures of perception. They gather and feed us continual and necessary information on a conscious and subconscious level that enables us to interpret and navigate the world and our experiences. We rely on our senses for survival, and yet we tend to take them for granted. Our senses are excellent guides to help bring us back to the present moment. When you're feeling lost or out of touch with yourself, come back to your senses. Tune in to what you can see, smell, hear, taste, or touch. Doing so will help ground you in the here and now. Feel your feet on the ground and your body supported by whatever you're sitting or lying on. Listen to the sounds around you: birdsong, rain, machinery, traffic, voices. Feel the temperature of your skin: warm, cool, clammy, dry. Breathe in the scent of where you are: coffee, toast, pine trees. Look around you, simply allowing your eyes to take in colors and shapes, light and shadow. Lick your lips and taste whatever you find there, sweet or salty. Say hello to everything, without judgment or the need to change or fix it, just hello.

 **INVITATION:** Focus on one sense at a time. Close your eyes (except for when you're focusing on sight), and put all your attention on that one sense, allowing it to grow and amplify. Be curious. What do you notice? What information comes to you through this particular sense?

 **JUST WRITE!** Take your time and tune in to each sense, one at a time, and write about what you experience in this moment through each of your senses. You can also write about any of the ideas in the sense categories below, imagining into each one, or you can make up your own!

**Sight:** Write about the sight of the sky at sunrise or sunset, snow falling, a flock of birds, a garden of flowers, mountains, a bustling city, a junkyard, a whale breaching, a child playing.

**Smell:** Write about the smell of burnt toast, the ocean, your grandparents' home, the air just before it rains, your pet, a person you like, your favorite restaurant, a campfire, cookies baking.

**Sound:** Write about the sound of wind, a dog howling, a sports event, your parents talking in another room, music, your friend's laughter, rain, the first sounds of morning, someone crying.

**Taste (sweet, sour, bitter, spicy, savory):** Write about the taste
of butter, an egg, honey, lemon, coffee, chocolate, salsa,
fresh-baked bread, ice cream, ripe strawberries.

**Touch:** Write about the feeling of walking barefoot on grass,
sand, snow, or hot pavement. A wool sweater or furry
slippers. Warm wind on your skin. The itch of a bug bite.

## Examples

*Sound: Serenade of Silence — Natalie, 14*

Night brings the serenade of silence.
The end of chirping, swooping birds
and the swish of speckled trees.
The silence sings.

No more stunning sunsets
swirling pink and purple chords.
The buzzing of bees, gone.
Taking their golden notes
of syrup with them.

The sky no longer dances.
The sun no longer sings.
The serenade of silence
is the music of night.

*Taste: Electric Lemon — Zane, 14*

Electric awakening
bat to ball

fireworks
screeching tires
silence my ranting
a searing brand
burning my tongue
contorting my face into a monster mask
sending cataclysms through my body
freezing my daydreams dead in their tracks
the trumpet of a lemon.

*Touch: The Breeze — Shawn, 16*

The breeze skims
across my skin
scalloping my surface
like a lake.
I ripple above
while down below
creatures swim
beating against my legs
as they climb up
to feed in the sun.
My skin is sprinkled
with stars.

## Spice It Up!

Let's have some fun with herbs and spices! Have you ever smelled something that catapulted you into a memory? It's a survival mechanism that smells are linked to the part of our brains that store memory. If we smell or taste something we learned is poisonous, we'll know not to eat it again. Similarly, we're wired for sweets. Sweet implies calories, which we need to survive, so when we smell and taste something sweet, we instinctively want more. Scent is special. It has the power to summon memories, feelings, and connections.

 INVITATION: Go to the kitchen and grab five to ten jars of herbs and spices. Choose some you like and some you're not so crazy about. If you can do this with a friend or group, it's fun to hide the label names. Important: don't try to figure out and name each spice; rather, focus on where the scent takes you in terms of memories, feelings, images, connections.

 JUST WRITE! Open the jars one by one. Notice the scent, color, texture. Describe the smell. This is not so easy. What does the scent evoke in you? Where does it take you? Is this an old familiar place or a new imagined place? Catch your mind wanting to figure out and name the spice, and instead focus on your feelings, impressions, and experience of the smell. Write about what it stirs up in you. Where does it take you?

## Examples

*Anise — Lev, 18*

Saltwater taffy
black licorice
pungent darkness
each spike of seeds
cartwheeling

through a dark
lifeless garden.

*Nutmeg — Lev, 18*

Hot and crisp
freeze-dried
icy center
breaks your teeth
yellow dust
following the car
through the desert
to the withered springs.

## Synesthesia

*Morning tastes of honeydew and the fading of candles.*
*It tastes of green honey and spring.*
— AMAL EL-MOHTAR, *The Honey Month*

Synesthesia is the blending of senses. The word *synesthesia* comes from the Greek *syn* for "together" and the root *aisthe* for "to feel." It is a condition that happens when one sense, such as sight, triggers another sense, such as smell, at the same time. For someone with *synesthesia*, each letter of the alphabet might have a different odor or color. Sound can be perceived and interpreted as light, and light patterns can evoke musical tones. How fun!

 INVITATION: Imagine you have synesthesia, a blending of the senses. How do you perceive the world through your blended senses?

JUST WRITE! Allow your mind to bend, your senses to blend, and your imagination to explore freely as you answer any or all of the following Synesthesia Questions. Write about one question at a time, each section at a time, or just choose the questions that spark you and combine a few of your answers to write a poem. Have fun, and get creative.

### • Synesthesia Questions •

What is the taste of anger or fear or joy?
What does blue or green or yellow taste like?
What does morning taste like?

What is the smell of excitement or sadness or desire?
What does disappointment smell like?
What is the smell of the color purple or orange?

What color or shape is sadness or hurt or love?
What is the color or shape of noise or quietude?
What color or shape is sleep or sleeplessness?

What texture is turquoise or silver or red?
What is the texture of need or loneliness or peace?
What texture is being asleep or wide awake?

What is the sound of sunshine or snow or midnight?
What is the sound of yellow or blue or pink?
What is the sound of love or loneliness?

## Examples

*Guilt — Katie, 19*

Guilt tastes like a sour parasite
weaseling its way into your fragile brain
It is the deafening yell that gets louder with time
rotting away at any semblance of sanity

Guilt tastes like a dumbbell
that slowly sinks to the bottom of your stomach
Every day the weight grows heavier
Your back gives out
because no one has the strength to carry
such crippling darkness

Guilt tastes like rusty nails
You know they serve no purpose
but that doesn't stop them from hurting
scraping your throat until it's raw
so that even the loudest scream
can only be heard as a whisper

*Pain — Ryka, 12*

Pain tastes like a lollypop that coats your tongue
with a bitter sour paste that never rubs off

Pain tastes like the thick layer of white fluff
splattering like a deformed sponge

Pain's taste increases and falls
leaving your mouth dull with punishment

Pain tastes like a thick dry powder
that fills your mouth with breathless suffering

Pain tastes like a soft mush that has no flavor
and discolors the world around you

darkening and damping your senses
until there is nothing left to resurrect.

# 6

# The Five W's

*The universe is made of stories,*
*not of atoms.*
— MURIEL RUKEYSER, "The Speed of Darkness"

Borrowing from journalism, let's apply the Five W's, the five basic questions to get to the heart of a story: who, what, when, where, why. We'll use these as points of entry to gather information, notice details, imagine possibilities. Since we are working with our intuition and imagination rather than solid facts, what we notice will reveal as much about us as it does about our subject. Pay attention. Sometimes it helps to squint your eyes to see between the lines.

## Photos and the Five W's

*To be a person is to have a story to tell.*
— ISAK DINESEN

I have always been intrigued with black-and-white photographs, and the work of photographers such as Mary Ellen

Mark, Sally Mann, Louis Hine, Annie Leibovitz. I see faces, stark and haunting, needing, loving, hurt or happy, and human, staring directly at me through the camera's eye. I always wonder, who are these people? What kind of life did they live? What did they struggle with? What broke them? How did they find the strength to get back up? Were they in love? Sometimes it seems as if they are seeing me as much as I am seeing them. What does it feel like to be witnessed, seen, revealed? Let's use the Five W's to discover or imagine the story in the photo.

 INVITATION: Gather evocative photos of people. Cut them out of magazines, use old postcards, or look in photography art books. Find some black-and-white photos, which tend to draw you in and reveal the soul of a person. Close-ups, face shots, oddly intriguing or striking-looking people will get your creative juices flowing. The more interesting the faces, poses, clothing, or relationships between the people, the better.

 JUST WRITE! Choose one of the photos, and use your imagination to answer the Five W's about the person or people in the photo. *Who* are they? *What* is going on, what's the story here? *When* is this taking place? *Where* are they? *Why* is this happening? You can also put yourself in the photo and write about the imagined relationship you have with the person or people, how you came to be together in this moment, what you're doing, and what the story is.

## Example

*Where Am I? — Sophie, 14*

Rugged designs trace the circle of charred wood
crumbling and leaving dark marks on the ground
Maybe one day she'll understand
She looks up at the fiery sky, strands of clouds like veins
The char disintegrates in her palm, leaving a ghostly
    smudge
Circles. More and more circles, she thinks to herself
"You see!" she yells at the sky
Burning wood makes char, and char writes on wood
and the wood becomes notes that try to explain to me
    where I am
"Where am I?"
She shovels her toes deeper into the dry ground
growing more frustrated with every passing second
No, she isn't oblivious
The most heart-wrenching part of her story
is the fact that she knows exactly where she is
The clearer section of sky
the part not obscured by smoke
gives her a perfect view of the earth
It stands directly in front of her
The vibrant green land
the glorious blue oceans
the wispy clouds

But today, she wakes on a dying planet
She knows she'll have a life without purpose

Long ago, the earth formed
and all the impossible puzzle pieces connected so
    beautifully
but now a chunk of rock has broken off
and it's floating farther and farther away
until the earth is nothing but a dot in a cold universe
Oh, she knows exactly where she is

### Postcard Poems

With current technology making communication instantaneous from any place in the world to another, we rarely send or receive postcards anymore. Postcards were so much fun. They were the pictures and messages we sent our family and friends from the places we traveled to on vacation and for work. When I was a little girl, I loved looking at the postcards my mother received from her friends all over the world. I would use the information on the postcards to make up my own stories, pretending I was the traveler.

 INVITATION: Gather a bunch of postcards or art cards. Choose three to five cards you feel an affinity with. Look through the cards until an idea or feeling comes to you about the people or scenery on the cards. What they are doing? What's the story? Apply the Five W's. Can you weave together the various pictures? Perhaps there is a similar theme, such as ocean, animals, flowers, people, or sights from other countries. Each card might carry a piece of the puzzle. For example, there could be a person on one card, a boat on another, and an abstract painting on the

third, and from these, an idea arises that this person is travel-
ing on the boat to visit the artist who painted the picture, and
they meet and fall in love, or not. It's up to you. Anything goes!

 JUST WRITE! Be curious. Use any clues you notice
on the cards such as the stamp, the date, and the
address. Read the message, if there is one, written
on the back of the card. Use any or all of these details to inform your ideas, and write a poem based on the information
you gather from the cards.

## Example

*The Old Man — Robert, 14*

On July 23, an old man sat
listening to the moon
he heard it howling
       crying for its mother.

The old man went to the town square
and walked past a white marble fountain
he put his feet in the fountain
       to cool off before lunch.

He spent the rest of the day
sitting by the fountain
feeding pigeons
       and talking to tourists.

When night came
he went to the theater
and completely forgot
    about the moon's crying.

Later, at home in bed, he listened
and found that the moon had stopped crying.
The old man smiled
    at his secret power.

## Morning News

The newspaper is a revealing record of who we are and how we function as a society. It reports the best and the worst of us: our wars, our crimes against ourselves and each other, personal and public injustices, scientific and artistic accomplishments, inventions, sports, entertainment, current trends, items of human interest, politics, personal opinions. Some mornings the news makes me cry. I always wonder why the majority of articles are about tragedy and misfortune and what this does to our understanding of the human condition. How does this affect our self-concept and our perspective of ourselves in relation to others? Does it help us to see our commonalities and have greater compassion for one another, or does it perpetuate an us-or-them ethos? What would it be like to have a whole newspaper focused on our victories, shared accomplishments, and acts of kindness?

INVITATION: Read through a newspaper, a magazine, or an internet newsfeed. Choose something that catches your attention. It could be a photo, an advertisement, a news article, an obituary, a want ad.

 JUST WRITE! Using the information provided in the graphic or text you chose, apply the Five W's and write about the feelings and images that arise in response to what you see or read. It can be something you learn or something you imagine about the people involved; or you can relate it to your own life.

## Example

*Mama Simba — Olivia, 14*

I am Mama Simba, people lover.
In life I value many things
but my family always comes first.
Here in Botswana,
we don't live a charmed life.
But that doesn't matter to me.
The happiness of my children and my husband
is what matters most.
Color fills my life.
It lifts me up when I am down.
The whole world around me is full of life and color.
It keeps me feeling good.
I am the village teacher

in a one-room schoolhouse.
All the children flock here
to learn and play together.
Today I am journeying
for food, money, and more work.
My brother comes with me.
We will do whatever it takes
to make ends meet.
To save our family
to save the schoolhouse
to save the community.
I will fight for what is right.
I will fight for what is necessary.

And one day, when I am no longer here,
I hope these battles will no longer be needed.
I hope there will be no more war,
no more anger, no more greed.
Just peace, happiness, and harmony.
I am Mama Simba, people lover.

## Still Life

One of the first things I learned in drawing class is to observe. Before you sketch, hash, shade, paint, or blend, you
simply observe. Let your eye follow the lines, witness the
natural relationships between shapes, and understand the
conversation between form and space. Only then can you do
justice to what you are capturing on paper. Let's see if we can
do this with our poetry.

INVITATION: Collect an assortment of objects such as an apple, a pinecone, a glass figurine, a flute, a shell, a feather, a toothbrush, a small potted plant, an old book, a toy plane, a seedpod, a crystal. Grab anything that calls to you. The weirder or even the more ordinary, the better. Arrange the objects on a table. Now take some time to simply observe these objects. What do they really look like? If you're looking at an apple, don't think about what you know an apple looks like; rather, look at *this* apple, and experience its *appleness*. What relationships do you notice between the different objects? What conversations are happening between space and form? To enrich your experience of the objects, you might want to touch some of them, feel their texture and weight. Use beginner's mind, as if this were the first time you are experiencing this object. Smell some of the objects, such as the apple, the old book, or whatever objects you have chosen. Explore all the objects in relation to one another, or single out a few that really speak to you.

 JUST WRITE! Look at the objects, and apply the Five W's until you feel you know the story of each shape, color, texture, curve, and shadow. Get a feel for the story of the relationship between the objects. Write about the objects as though you were sketching them for an art class. As if seeing them for the first time, allow the objects to reveal themselves to you. Let them tell their story, and perhaps more of your own story.

## Example

*Still Life Comes to Life — Amelia, 15*

She puts a seashell to my ear
I smile as the tides echo through my head.
She wears an amethyst pendant
crowns me with a circlet of pinecones
and a wreath of beads washed up from a boat
that sank ages ago.

She puts a bird's nest in my palm
and I feel the coarse weave
constructed from days of constant work
by two feathered sprites.
I did not hear their songs.

Her teeth crunch into a red apple
juice running down her chin.
She smells of salt and bones
washed clean by the sea.
She turns to me with ocean on her lips
and makes me see.

She turns my head to watch the sun bleed
slowly into the waves.
She is the Queen of Spades
a playing card washed onshore
that I pick up and put in my pocket
and later place under my pillow
to dream.

# 7

# Muse of the Ordinary

*Make the ordinary come alive....*
*The extraordinary will take care of itself.*
— WILLIAM MARTIN, *The Parent's Tao Te Ching*

We can find poetry everywhere, if we know how to look and how to listen. Poetry lives in the simplest things, in the *is-ness* of an object, in the relationship between people, in nature, in light and shadow, in the truth of our feelings. We can invite our muse to inspire us by calling forth poetry from ordinary sources that are part of our everyday lives, such as a dictionary entry, a to-do list, a letter, an event announcement, a horoscope, even a magic spell!

 INVITATION: Refer to the Ordinary Sources below. Choose one you may not have considered poetic, like a horoscope or a to-do list or even a dictionary entry. Perhaps you don't come in contact with a magic spell every day, but maybe it's time to try your hand at writing one!

**JUST WRITE!** Write a poem in the form you chose. Or take a poem you've already written and try adapting it into that form.

## · *Ordinary Sources* ·

A letter
A horoscope
A dictionary entry
A magic spell
A to-do list
An event announcement

## Examples

*My Horoscope — Olivia, 14*

The EARTH
without art
is just
EH!
Hello Guardian
Choose Spirit
Embrace Passion
Love!
Taste
the arts
within.
Goodness, Gracious!

*EXPLORE*
   *SPLASH*
      *ADVENTURE*
Feed the world
with a thousand
W O R D S.
Come as you are.
Leave as you want to be.
Stay GOLD!


*To-Do List — Jade, 13*

Paint the sky
Sing to the stars
Comb the grass
Feed the flowers
Tame the lions
Weave a dress of spider silk
Cut firewood for the sun
Read stories to the children


*Magic Spell — Izzy, 18*

Fang of wolf
and ink of squid
mend my broken heart whole
like when I was a kid

Dew of moss
and baleen of whale

the old story changes now
into a bright new tale

Through darkness, through illness
I've grown strong and true
the one I've been looking for
is me, not you

Pearl of shell
and breath of ghost
I draw to my life
what I love most

With heart of love
and voice of song
friends now gather
and to each other, we belong

Lover of sea
and sky and earth
today is the beginning
of my rebirth

Lover of quiet
and dark and deep
I am a treasure
for myself to keep.

## Blackouts!

Working with words that are already there can bring out a whole new kind of poem. Poetry magnets that stick to your refrigerator are great for this. Cutting words out of magazines or newspapers and piecing them together is another great way to call up new poems. With blackouts, we'll take a page from a book, circle the words we like, and use a marker to black out the parts we don't want, leaving a poem in our wake. For presents to give to my students one year, I bought a stack of old books at the thrift store on subjects I knew they'd like: fantasy, animals, anatomy, sports, cooking, and of course, literature. Their summer poetry homework was to take the book with them on vacation and make blackout poems through the entire book.

 INVITATION: Get an old book or some pages from a magazine or newspaper. You'll need a pencil with an eraser and a thick black marker, like a Sharpie.

 JUST WRITE! Read through the pages and choose one with words that catch your eye. With a pencil, circle the words in the text that jump out at you. Then, using your Sharpie, black out all the other words so the remaining words you circled create a poem. The poem may not always make the kind of linear sense you're used to. Be open to experimenting and creating a new kind of poem, one you have to stretch your mind to understand.

## Examples

*by Jasmine, 16*

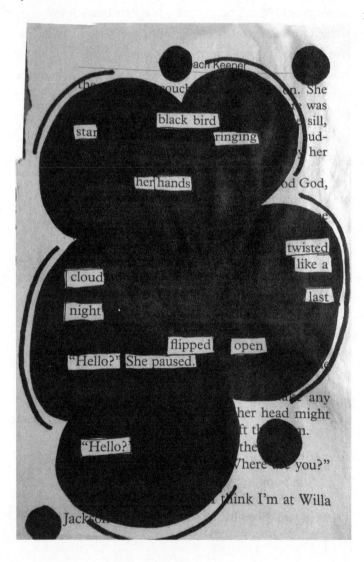

*by Enzo, 15*

*by Noelle, 13*

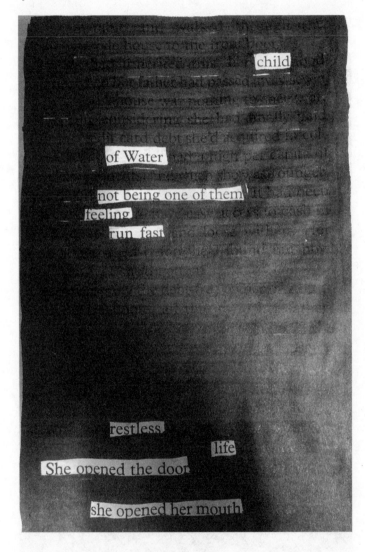

child

of Water

not being one of them

feeling

run fast

restless

life

She opened the door

she opened her mouth

*by Leena, 18*

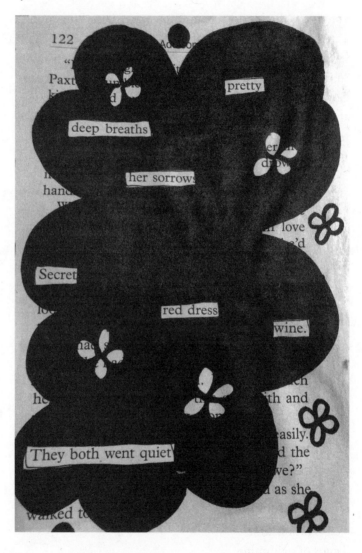

## Recipe Poems

You know the kind I mean: "How to Write a Blues Song": 4 cups sorrow, 2 Tbsp. regret, ½ cup of starry night, 1 oz. forgiveness, and a dash of passion. Mix all ingredients until smooth. Bring to a boil, then simmer on stove for 7 hours. Cover and let cool. Pour over a bed of sweet sliced promises and garnish with chili pepper flakes. Serve in one big bowl with two spoons. Eat at midnight.

 **INVITATION:** Think about all the elements that go into cooking your favorite meals. Consider ingredients, measurements, preparation, utensils. Do you boil, bake, sauté, steam, roast, grill, stir, blend? How long do you cook the dish for, and at what temperature? How do you serve it? Just as you do with cooking, get creative!

 **JUST WRITE!** Write a recipe for how to heal a broken heart, how to make a little brother invisible, how to make someone fall in love with you, how to create world peace or end human suffering. Anything is possible. Cook up a storm!

## Examples

*How to Make Happiness — Leo, 13*

5 cups of sunshine
4 cups of swimming
3 cups of adventure novels

2 cups of music
1 cup of friends

Fry the sunshine and swimming together in a pan with butter.
Grill the adventure novels until tender.
Blend the music with ice.
Toast the friends lightly.
Mix all of these together until creamy.
Put in a muffin tin and bake at 700° for two days and two
　　　nights.
When the smell makes your mouth water, take out and
　　　sprinkle with snowflake frosting.
Serve on a colorful plate.

*Peace o' Cake — Mila, 11*

Take your kindness and add two spoons of it and melt it all
Take your eggs and mash them up
Add a drizzle of understanding, and a pinch of sugar
Throw in a cup of flour, bake at 300°
Take it out at midnight when your hope is the most hopeful
　　　it will ever be
Take your enemy by the hand and help them take it out of
　　　the oven
Let it cool and grab a slice
As you eat the first bite, the internal war ends
Let the peace settle in

## Secret Weapon: 7 × 7

On good days our writing comes pouring out of us, and we can't stop and we don't want to, but other times, even though we want to write, we can't find our voice or our starting point. We can't find the way in. When I'm having trouble getting the poetry to flow, I use my secret weapon! I pull the seventh book off my bookshelf, open it to page 7, and write down the words from the seventh line, no matter how weird or out of context. I use these words as the first line of my poem to get me started or as the last line that I build up to. You can create any structure you want for this.

 **INVITATION:** Go to your bookshelf and choose the seventh book. Open it to page 7. Look at the seventh line on the page. Whatever it says, write it down. Use either the whole sentence or just a few of the words.

 **JUST WRITE!** Begin a poem using this line or a few of these words, and see where it takes you. Limit the length of the poem to seven lines. Try this as many times as you like. Set up your own parameters, using your favorite number.

### Example

*By Way of the Invisible — Jasmine, 18*

By way of the invisible
I found the monarchs

hanging from the big tree
over the bridge
like a million flower petals
their fragile bodies
fan the sky.

## Lyrical Muse

As a singer-songwriter, I've learned to respect the mystical process involved in writing a song. Though I am fully present and pouring myself into a song when I'm writing it, I'm also aware that there is something bigger than just me at play. Meet the muse in the music. Her name is Lyric. If you open to her and ask for her help, she will plant ideas in your brain, light a fire in your fingers, and stir emotion in your heart. Song lyrics are poetry. Within the magic of a song, the lyrics express thoughts and feelings, marrying them to rhythm and melody. Music brings poetry to life.

 **INVITATION:** Let's dip into this accessible form of poetry that we come in contact with every day in the music we listen to and love. Think about a song you like, and choose your favorite line from the song. Your favorite might change tomorrow or next week, but for right now, choose a song and some lyrics that speak to you.

 **JUST WRITE!** Use this lyric as the first line of your poem. Try weaving it through your piece a couple of times, repeating it like the chorus of a song. Be willing to go anywhere this lyric takes you. Let the lyrical muse inspire you. Stay curious. Be ready for anything! Like any good muse, she may lead you on a wild adventure that takes you to somewhere wholly new.

## Example

*The Day I Start Living — Libby, 19*

Today I lifted my head up high
I saw a blue sky with wings
following the sun with a sigh
*This is the day I start living*

The sky is laughing from its eyes
its voice is a golden harp singing

Show me how to laugh and sing
I begged the great blue sky
Show me how to love again
*This is the day I start living*

## Write a Song with Rhythm and Rhyme

*After silence, that which comes nearest to expressing the inexpressible is music. Music is what feelings sound like.*
— ALDOUS HUXLEY, *Music at Night*

I love this question: "Can you imagine a world without music?" The moment I try to imagine it, everything in the world collapses and implodes. I simply cannot imagine it.

Can you? Music is life! I've been singing since before I could speak. Music is my mother tongue; it's how I express the feelings that are beyond words. For most of us, music is woven into the fabric of our lives. We have a soundtrack for the best and worst times. We turn to music to celebrate and to soothe. We respond to the rhythmic and melodic language of music with our bodies, hearts, and souls. Music is a language before words. It is pure feeling, and in music we find belonging — to ourselves and something bigger than ourselves.

### Rhythm and Rhyme

Most songs follow a pattern of rhythm and rhyme. An easy pattern to start with is a folk song, a ballad, or the blues. They usually have four lines per verse and follow a rhyming pattern of AABB or ABAB, meaning either the first two and/or last two lines rhyme, or the first and third and/or the second and fourth lines rhyme.

 INVITATION: Choose a musical genre such as pop, folk, rock, blues, country, reggae, rap, hip-hop, and so forth. Choose a topic such as being lovestruck, heartbreak, a social issue, a rant. Listen to your favorite songs and notice the issues they address, the rhythmic pattern they follow, how the melody expresses emotion. See if you can copy it. Or try the AABB or ABAB pattern, or create your own.

 JUST WRITE! Write the song lyrics for any music genre you want. As you're writing the song, keep saying or singing it out loud so you hear the rhythm pattern as you go. Stick with it. Believe in your song.

## Examples

*Night Owl — Colette, 17*

The song of summer
and the silver stream
the light of the moon
shining into my dream

The call of the night owl
up in her tree
three times she asks
who who who could it be?

I know in my heart
she's calling to me
so I rise on dark wings
and set myself free

*Today — Rich, 16*

Today the sky is full of gray
my heart is raining too
I'll reach inside the sun's golden head
and pull out a sky of blue

## Wild Words

Wild words pop up like wildflowers where you least expect them. They sparkle in the corner of your eye or sing in the corner of your ear. You may pass one in a sign on the wall, you may find one jumping off the page of a book, or you may catch one in an overheard conversation. It can be a word or phrase that just pops into your head from out of the blue, wherever or whatever that is! These are words that grab your attention, words that jump in your pocket and want you to take them home with you. Perhaps it's a word you've never heard, an odd or funny phrase, or a word you just like the sound and taste of when you chew it in your mouth.

 INVITATION: Gather ten to twenty wild words or phrases. Sit with each one like a treasure or the last of the summer blackberries. Be sure to write these words down; remember, they are wild, and if you don't write them down, they will gallop off to the next adventure. Collect your wild words or phrases in a basket, box, or jar over the course of a day or a week. Write your wild words on little slips of paper and slide them into your container. Let them marinate.

 JUST WRITE! When you have ten to twenty wild words or phrases, take them out, one at a time, and start arranging them like stringing the beads of a necklace. Feel free to add any words you need to make your poem. Sometimes the best poems wander off the beaten path. Allow the wild words to stretch your imagination and take you somewhere wild and new. Highlight your wild words by writing them in a different color or a different font. You can even glue them right onto your page, like a collage.

## Example

*Wild Words — Kimberly, 19*

I gathered *raw cacao* and a *song of silence*
and put them in a *frying pan* with some butter.
I needed to *arrive 30 to 40 minutes before the performance*
so I boarded my *seaplane*
and piloted toward *the silk road.*
But suddenly, I knew what I really needed:
I needed to *fuel my passion.*
I was knee-deep in *ecopsychology,*
halfway through a *mud mask* that felt like *broken glass,*
and almost out of *vitamin-rich protein powder,*
when *wishful thinking* helped me to realize
I can turn this plane around.
I can head directly to my hometown of *Monterey,*
wrap myself in *above fair-trade organic cotton* pajamas,
just in time to absorb the peace and colors of the sunset
      through *osmosis.*
No longer does her *Private Property* sign deter me.
In fact, *Can you believe she would say that?!*
Or that I'd ever listen?
Heck, *I recycle and reuse.*
I am powerful.
I carry my own *atlas.*
My heart is my *compass.*
*I can fly!*

## • 8 •

# Ode à la Mode

*I resisted the mad impulse to put them
in a golden cage and each day give them
birdseed and pieces of pink melon.*
— PABLO NERUDA, "Ode to My Socks"

What's an ode? *Ode* comes from the Greek word meaning "song." An ode is a lyric poem, a tribute, a song, a praise, a celebration. I love odes. My students love odes. They can dream up a hundred different ways to celebrate a color, an item of clothing, a piece of fruit, or a vegetable. When in doubt, write an ode. You can write an ode to just about anything!

## Power Clothing

It might sound silly, but have you ever put on an item of clothing and suddenly felt like you ruled the world? Maybe it's your favorite pair of jeans, a pair of old cowboy boots, a hand-me-down jacket, a vintage hat. You put it on and, suddenly, you have the power! I have this brown leather vest with a fur collar. When I put it on, I am transformed into a warrior woman. I can accomplish anything I set out to do when I wear this vest. What item of clothing do you have that helps you rule the world or even just makes you feel safe and comfy, like you belong?

 INVITATION: Think about your favorite item of clothing, the one that makes you feel your best — safe, comfortable, invincible, like you're on fire!

 JUST WRITE! Write an ode, a tribute, a song of praise to this item of clothing. Combine your imagination with real-life experiences for unique details that will bring your poem to life.

## Examples

*Ode to My Scarf — Nicole, 15*

Velvet snake
  Wrapped around my shoulders
   Crawls up my neck
    Protecting me from evil
     And the biting chill that creeps
      Down my back and brings
      Sickness to my body
      Scented deeply
     A field of wildflowers
    Can't stop smelling it
   Every chance I get
All for this one feeling
Like symphonies
  And ecstasy

My body unravels
 My naked neck reveals
  The kissing room
   Where night consumed me
    And fingers teased
     I wrap my hand
      Around the velvet creases
     Of perfect memories
    Those deviled kisses
With a French accent.


*Running Shoes — Kobe, 16*

I bought these running shoes
for myself
A couple of dune buggies
ripped and wet
From running in rainy weather
like squeaky stairs
Every step I take
sounds like an out-of-tune guitar
Together,
we run to our dreams.


## Color Crazy

*Color is a power that directly influences the soul.*
— WASSILY KANDINSKY, *A Revolution in Painting*


Have you ever noticed how color influences the way you feel? Have you ever walked into a room painted blue and suddenly felt ill? Does the color tan make you tired? Are you a person who wears only black? I go through phases when I cannot bear bright colors. But then something shifts, my mood changes, and I can't get enough purple, orange, and turquoise in my life. It's as if there are nutrients in these colors that my brain and body need. One time I was at a yard sale and saw a table painted a shade of turquoise that I simply could not live without. I asked the woman what color it was, and she said Caribbean Blue and directed me to the paint store around the corner. It was like mood food. I bought a can and painted all the furniture in my cottage Caribbean Blue. Certain colors give me a headache, like bright yellow and neon green. Other colors make me feel calm and peaceful, like peach and pale pink. I like the spaciousness of white and the warmth of cream. Gray makes me depressed. Are you sensitive to color? Do certain colors influence your mood? Do they drain or energize you?

 INVITATION: Think about which colors feed you and which deplete you. Which colors most express who you are and how you feel? Do different colors match different colors match different moods? Which colors are you drawn to, and which are you repelled by? Are there colors you absolutely need and others you cannot tolerate?

 JUST WRITE! Choose a color you resonate with, and write an ode to this color, a song of praise and celebration. Use detail, memories, items you have that are this color, and actual experiences that help you express your affinity for this color. Have fun!

## Example

*Ode to Yellow — Amelia, 15*

Yellow, my lost love.
In your pointed shoes
and great capes of chick feathers
leaving a trail of pale fairy dust.
You, the color that initiates rust
tarnishes silver, and ages barbed wire.
Not true!
Lies cast by your older, uglier stepsisters,
Orange and Red
who fed you sour melon until you were sick.
You are the forgotten daughter.
Forgotten even by me
for I was so caught by Red's shocking and fatal beauty
that I paid no attention to you.
Yellow, I miss your hands of light.
You are nomadic,
you have moved so many times
I can no longer find you.
But it was near a stream
of aspens and rabbits, and blooming daffodils.
You, looking like the queen of the dryads.
We spoke, for one cannot help but speak in your presence.
Yellow, with your calm radiance, your listening ear.
I sobbed, and you held me in your arms
my shudders shaking us both.
You brought me back to life.
I was embarrassed to have fallen
so deeply for you.

## Fruit and Veggies

Just because you've eaten hundreds of apples, thousands of bananas, and millions of baby carrots doesn't mean you've ever really looked at them, or thought about them, or tasted them, as a poet. So, with beginner's mind, as if for the first time, as if you have just arrived on an alien planet, meet this fruit or vegetable.

 INVITATION: Grab a piece of fruit or a vegetable, and take some time to really explore it. Use beginner's mind. Notice the shape, color, smell, texture, contour. Cut it in half. Look at the seeds or the pit. Take out the seeds or pit and look at the space they used to inhabit. Explore the landscape and architecture of this fruit or veggie. And finally, taste it!

 JUST WRITE! Write an ode to celebrate this unique fruit or vegetable. Use your senses. Let your imagination cut loose on this one. The weirder, the better. Make it silly, sensual, sad, sarcastic. Make it your own!

## Examples

*Ode to a Pear — Ava, 13*

Sometimes she wants to clothe herself
in a strong skin
carved out of soft, speckled jade.

She wants to wear it like armor
built of lacquered plates, strung together.

She wants her words to have a crisp bite
she can sink her teeth into
feel the ivory bone dive into a juicy core.

She wants to taste the fresh, green whiff
of growing when she speaks.

She wants to keep her pearlescent heart
with its streaming seeds safe.
So she does.

### Cucumber Ode — Austin, 16

Ah, cucumber, my small green boat
sliding down the Amazon River
seeds like cells like blood like eggs
crispy and crunchy and quenching
on this hot summer day
searching for toads
with blue-striped backs
my cone-shaped hat
my pants that wrap
complete to eat
with skin and seeds and flesh
I carry you with me
my friend
so fresh.

## Soul Food

You know that food you've just got to have, that food you crave when you've had a bad day or want to celebrate an accomplishment, that food that just makes everything right with the world, that food that gets into your soul and makes you sing?

 **INVITATION:** Think about the food you go to when you need comfort, a sense of home or belonging, the food you ask for to celebrate your birthday. Maybe it's mac and cheese or a burger; maybe it's lasagna or your mom's fried chicken; maybe it's fresh-baked banana bread or strawberry ice cream. You know what I'm talking about!

 **JUST WRITE!** Write an ode to your soul food, that food that makes your heart beat, your soul sing.

## Example

*My Mom's Corn Bread — Nai'a, 12*

My mom's corn bread
is as soft and fluffy as a moon bed
bright-yellow like sunshine
with pieces of opal glowing
from an inner force
and so delicious you could get sick
from eating the whole pan of it

I ask for it on my birthday
I ask for it when I'm feeling down
I ask for it when I can't sleep

I ask for it when nothing else
in the whole world
will quench my hunger
I ask for it warm
with lots of butter

My mom's corn bread
could cure the sick
feed all the hungry children
heal up broken hearts
and put joy back into people
who have lost their way

My mom's corn bread
is magic.

# • 9 •

# Shape-Shift

*The Irish believed that gods, druids, poets, and others in
touch with the magical world could be literal shape-shifters.*
— THOMAS CAHILL, *How the Irish Saved Civilization*

From what I understand about physics, everything is made
of energy. We may look solid, but we're actually gazil-
lions of vibrating electrons. So, using our imagination, we
can shape-shift our energy to become anything we want, to
tap into and harness the energy of water, fire, a mountain,
a storm, sunshine, darkness, sadness, joy; you name it, you
can become it. Imagination makes us fluid and flexible. It
dissolves our boundaries. It allows us freedom. Knowing we
can shape-shift and become anything we want, we are limit-
less; we are magic. Let's try shape-shifting. Imagine you are
water, deep and blue, with many moods. How do you feel,
and what do you know about yourself as water? Or become
fire: I am born from a single spark; I consume everything in
my path. As fire, what is your purpose and wisdom, and who
are your friends?

INVITATION: Refer to the Shape-Shift Categories below. Choose one you relate to or want to explore from the elements, the weather, day and night, or feelings. Then take a look at the Shape-Shift Questions and consider what kind of personality, mood, characteristics, challenges, and dreams you have as this element, weather, day or night, or feeling. What hidden parts of you might it embody and express? What parts of you can come out and play when you shape-shift?

 JUST WRITE! Close your eyes and allow yourself to shape-shift, becoming the element, weather, day or night, or feeling of your choice. What are you wearing? How do you move? Where do you live? Who are your friends? What are your fears and dreams? For more ideas, refer to the Shape-Shift Questions below. Go wild!

### • Shape-Shift Categories •

**Elements:** earth, air, fire, water

**Weather:** rain, snow, wind, fog, thunderstorm, hurricane, tornado

**Day and Night:** Be specific about what time of day or night you're writing about.

**Feelings:** anger, sadness, jealousy, fear, confusion, desire, grief, insecurity, joy, sensuality, doubt, rage, hurt, guilt, inspiration, silence, compassion, wisdom, and more

## • *Shape-Shift Questions* •

Where was it born?

What does it look like?

What does it wear?

How old is it?

How does it move?

Where does it live?

What is its favorite season?

What does it struggle with?

What is it good at?

What is its work?

What is its hobby?

What does it like to eat?

What inspires it?

What instrument does it play?

What sports does it play?

What does it fear?

What does it want and need?

What is its wisdom or message?

Who are its friends and allies?

Who are its enemies?

What is its dream?

What is its mission?

What are the constructive and destructive aspects of it?

What is your relationship or connection with it?

## Examples

*Air — Ashtyn, 9*

I was born in wind
I wear the wind as a dress
It flows like water.
I eat the grass and live everywhere at once
I play the violin and dance on the water
I dream of being solid.
I keep you alive every day
You breathe me in and out
I wish I could be seen, but I am clear
I am air.


*Water — Lev, 18*

Knowing I'll get what I want
I buy a blue dress
wrap my black hair in linen
dark as night
lurk in murky water
all I have left
swallow, spit, grieve
drain in wet sorrow
mother to many
healer to few
my time has come
I lie on the ground
in vast dryness
an icy surface
I yearn to hear

a trickle
of dreams
quench me.


*Wind — Tess, 11*

I am the gentle breeze
and the catastrophic hurricane
I create the waves on the water
I make the fire stronger
As for the earth, I grant it seeds
In my light, white dress
I move the inky clouds
I fill the sails for merry, whistling sailors
I blow the balloons to the top of the sky
where I wait in hope
for the sun to set
for the moon to rise
I am wind.


*Daytime — Ashtyn, 9*

I am Daytime
High noon
I live in the sun's flames
I dance and sing all day
I never hide.
I let my light flow through the earth with love and peace
I wear a bright-yellow sundress, a tie-dyed shawl, and a
       wide-brim sunhat
I have wings bigger than the world.

*Night — Lila, 11*

I am night, 12 midnight
you might think that night has no color
but the sky is deep-navy
the oceans shine silver
in the glow of moon
and if you look closely
you might just see me
hair as dark as obsidian
skin as silver as the glistening stars
dress flowing in the cool night breeze
I like to pay visits to the moon
she often gets lonely
and if you're lucky
you might just catch me
You might think that night is silent
but you are mistaken
owls hoot
crickets chirp
and of course, there's me
I like to sing to the shining stars
in the cool night breeze
although you might miss me
for I am night
elusive and mysterious.

## Personification

If we can shape-shift our human form to become anything
we want, then we can also make things human that are not.

This is called *personification*, or giving human characteristics to something nonhuman. For example, working with the Shape-Shift Categories, we can take an element, the weather, day or night, or a feeling and turn it into a person. I love personification, and so do my students. It gives rise to playful poems that allow us to express parts of ourselves we often keep quiet. Imagine fire as an angry woman flashing through town in her red velvet dress, sparks flying as she speaks her mind. Imagine rain going for a walk and feeling so exhilarated she twirls until she's dizzy and falls down laughing. Imagine joy screaming down the street on his new yellow skateboard, leaving a trail of sunny graffiti wherever he goes.

 INVITATION: Refer again to the Shape-Shift Categories: elements, weather, day and night, or feelings, and choose one to personify, taking something nonhuman and making it human. Have fun with this! Try choosing one that could allow you to express parts of yourself you usually keep hidden.

 JUST WRITE! With your choice in mind, begin to envision it as a person. What would fire, water, earth, or air look like if it were a person? What would snow wear? How does rain speak? How does nighttime move? Where does sadness live? Who are joy's friends and enemies? For more ideas, refer again to the Shape-Shift Questions.

## Write from Different Points of View:
## First, Second, or Third Person

Personification is a great opportunity to experiment with writing from different perspectives. You can write in the first person, the *I/we* perspective; the second person, the *you* perspective; or the third person, the *he/she/it/they* perspective. If you usually write in first person, try writing in second or third. If you usually write in second or third person, try shape-shifting and write in first, becoming the element, weather, day and night, or feeling. Choose whichever one gives you greater access to your ideas and feelings.

### Examples

*Earth — Riva, 16*

Earth rolls into town
like she owns the place
dark-skinned and curvy
wearing nothing
but a leather minidress
her bare feet caked in mud
sunlight braids
her hazelnut hair
which dances down her waist
she gathers the wind
in her calloused hands
fills her pockets
with seeds that shine
smiles like she's got a secret

kneels down low to the ground
sings a song of thanks
presses her fingers into the soil
throws her head back laughing
as she's quickly swallowed up
and turned into compost.

### Fire — Daniel, 18

Fire is quiet or it can roar.
Maybe fire doesn't mean to destroy everything it touches,
    but it does.
Fire goes wherever it can, even when it's not wanted.
It dances in the air, and it needs air to exist.
Fire isn't scared of dying.
It lives knowing its death will come at any moment.
Fire looks like it wouldn't know how to control itself, but
    over time it learns when to cause chaos and when to be
    calm and easy, like slow dancing.
Even though fire destroys everything it touches, it learns
    how to be gentle with what it loves, so it can enjoy,
    savor the moment, and appreciate what it loves just a
    little bit longer.
Fire lives knowing that what it loves will eventually be no
    more and will never exist again for the rest of fire's
    existence, once it has been destroyed.

### Wildfire — Ava, 13

She moves fast. She combusts. She snags shreds of earth and
air on her sharp nails. She licks flames from her fingers. Swift

like a lion chasing its prey across the savanna, she's ruthless. Young and old all at once. She devours everything in her path, leaving the edges burnt and ragged. When she's had her fill and quenched her hunger, she slinks away, licking her chops. Only a smattering of ash remains, clean white freckles dusting her fur. Think she gives nothing? Take a closer look at the smoking trail her footprints leave behind. Here crimson poppies spring up in her wake. She'll give you peace, for a price.

### Anxiety — Clairrissa, 17

He lives in the darkest corner of my brain.
Next to his very best friend,
Fear.
He wears a black hoodie & red socks.
Wherever I go,
he follows.
He makes me quiet.
When he's around
I feel like a lost child.
He keeps me up all night.
In the morning,
when he's gone,
I'm at peace.

### Sadness — June, 15

Sadness wears his grandfather's
gray wool sweater
with elbow patches worn threadbare.

He goes for a long walk through town
at 4 a.m. on Christmas Eve
the lights humming
against a dark sky.
He listens to the sound of sleeping.
He puts his hand in his pocket
searching for warmth
pulls out a note
folded and yellowed with age.
It's from his sister, Understanding.
It says, dear brother
I remember when you were just a little boy
running around in the backyard
chasing fireflies.

# • 10 •

# Body Language

*I sing the body electric.*
— WALT WHITMAN, *Leaves of Grass*

Our bodies are miracles! Self-regulating, self-healing bio-machines. Instruments tuning us to the world through our senses. Bio-vehicles that walk, run, swim, dance, sit, work, sleep, eat, poop, touch, cuddle, and more. We can hurt, bruise, and break our bodies and, astonishingly, they repair themselves. They get sick and get healthy again. They grow and age, and eventually they die. Understandably, we identify with our bodies. They are our bio-homes. The way we feel about our bodies is written all over us. You can tell a lot about someone by the way they carry themselves: Are they guarded or open? Do they meet your eyes or not? Do they hunch their shoulders or stand tall? Do they hide or reveal themselves with their clothing?

Despite the great gift of our bodies, we waste a lot of energy judging them. How do we measure up? How do our bodies compare to other people's bodies? Are we thin enough, strong enough? Are we too tall or too short? Are we beautiful or good-looking enough? There is so much pressure in our culture to be thin, fit, and beautiful. How can we possibly make the cut and fit in without making ourselves crazy and possibly unhealthy? Can we find a way to accept and be grateful for our amazing bodies?

In this section I invite you to explore and write about your body, starting with your hands, skin, and belly, and moving into more sensitive areas. You have an opportunity to express your true feelings about your insecurities, gripes, prides, and pleasures about your body. We often feel shame about our bodies, and this makes us shut down to the beautiful gift they are. It helps to write down the bad feelings or say them out loud. It's liberating and healing to express our true feelings about our bodies.

Let's dispel the societal myths about what makes our bodies beautiful or not by finding our own reasons for beauty, based on how we feel rather than on how we look. And finally, let's move into loving and accepting our bodies. Try looking and feeling from the inside out, rather than from the outside in. Try imagining how you would relate to your body if you'd never seen another body to compare yourself to. Try imagining that you've never looked in a mirror, that your experience of your body is based solely on inhabiting it. You will have your body your whole life. I encourage you to love, celebrate, and care for the miracle of your beautiful body!

## Hands

Hands connect us to the world. They are an extension of our hearts. They open and close around what we keep and what we give. With our opposable thumbs, our hands are amazing and articulated tools that enable us to create and make anything we can imagine. We perform intricate tasks, build houses, make art, feed and clean ourselves, hold a baby, emphasize a point in a conversation, type, touch, pick things up, play an instrument, throw a ball. Hands, like people, come in all shapes and sizes. What do you do with your hands?

 INVITATION: Take some time to study hands, yours or someone else's. Consider everything you do with your hands. Can you imagine not having hands? Ever injured one of your hands, where you could only use the other one for a period of time? I have. Try using your nondominant hand for a whole day to write or draw or even brush your teeth.

 JUST WRITE! Write about hands. What are all the things you do with your hands? Write about the images, feelings, and associations that come to you when you think about your hands and everything you do with them all day long. For even more fun, ask yourself a question, and write the answer with your nondominant hand.

## Examples

*Hands — Jennaya, 15*

hands, you creatures. you long-fingered friends. searching out every notch to touch and taste with fingertips. you whisper songs on my body in the morning. you yawn and stretch.

curl back up to sleep more. but by midday you've found your voice.

you speak out loud. gesticulating. clap, snap, point, shake when you don't get your way. you don't believe a word I say. until you touch it. reach for your friend. take her hands in yours. an intimate meeting. like two people, the hands. door-ways. keys into the temple of another person.

I have felt you close in a fist. splay open in wonder. at your best, an invitation. you ask for more. or less. I've seen you end it with one quick sideways swipe universally recognized as NO! Stop. Enough! you are so quick to cover my mouth, hide my face. my laughter. my tears.

what to do with you when I speak in front of people? how to get you to sit quietly in my lap? yes, you fidget. you pick. you climb into my mouth. my hands. curious. skilled. my constant companions. my pets.

*Wave Hello, Wave Goodbye — Jacob, 16*

Speak under the table
in sign language
where no one can hear
spell letters on your palm

Seek out places
that are good
to hide
good to feel

Rings of silver
rings of gold
gypsy friends' fingers
flying on a dark guitar

Half-moons anchored
in nail-bed boats
sail home alone
after a night of shining

A warm hand takes mine
a secret is passed in braille
but gone too soon
wave hello, wave goodbye

## Skin

Our skin is the boundary between us and the world. Many
expressions in our language refer to skin: being comfortable in our own skin, someone or something getting under
our skin, something making our skin crawl, rubbing us the
wrong way. Certain emotions affect our skin by giving us
chills or goose bumps. Skin can be scratched, bruised, cut, or
burned, but it is very resilient; it regenerates, and most of us
have a few scars from when it was wounded and healed over.
As we age, our skin loses elasticity, and our faces become the
wrinkled road maps of our lives. Our skin tells the stories of
our journeys in scars, stretch marks, acne, tattoos, wrinkles.
What stories and poems are written on your skin?

INVITATION: Think about skin, yours or someone else's. What do you notice, without judgment? Be open to the stories and poems of someone's skin.

JUST WRITE! Tell the story about something that has left its mark on your skin. Do you have a scar from an accident or surgery? Do you have stretch marks from when you were growing or when you had a baby? Do you have a tattoo?

## Example

*Hummingbird — Elisa, 17*

They called me one when I was a little girl
I, who was always flittering around
light as a feather, determined as a bee
my eyes iridescent, my cheeks flushed
never could sit still
always dancing off
to the next sip of sweetness

So when I went off to art school
and all my friends
were decorating their skin with ink
I wanted one
on my left shoulder
so I could look back and remember

I didn't know it would hurt
the tiny wings

the red throat
the sound and breeze as they hovered
for one infinitesimal moment
with pointed beak

Supping up the midday mead
the circles they made in the air
chasing each other
drunk on a sunny day
above the pear tree
I wanted that kind of love

## Belly

You might not think so at first, but our belly is a place of power and wisdom. Our center of gravity is in our belly. In Chinese medicine and martial arts, the source of all our energy is located in our belly, about two inches below the navel. Western science says our belly is our second brain and is connected with as many neural pathways as the brain in our skull. We say we have butterflies in our stomach, a knot in our belly; we say quit your bellyaching, trust your gut. Does your stomach clench or relax in response to how you feel? Do you starve yourself or overeat in relation to your mood? Are you proud of your muscular six-pack and the sit-ups you do every morning, or do you wear loose shirts to hide the bulge? A vulnerable and possibly erotic place, our bellies. How about the terrain of our navels, where we were attached by umbilical cord to our mother's womb, like a piece of fruit attached to a tree? How do you feel about your belly? Are you in touch with the power and brain of your gut? Try some belly love: put your hands on your belly, and taking belly breaths, breathe in and out, letting your belly make contact with your hands, filling your hands on your in-breath. Say hello to your belly with your hands. Listen to your belly through your hands. What does it tell you? Thank your belly. Love your belly. Listen to the wisdom of your belly.

 **INVITATION:** Think about your relationship with your belly. Do you tend to stuff down challenging emotions, such as anger or sadness, and hold them in your belly? Do you trust your gut?

 **JUST WRITE!** Write about your belly. Express all the positive and negative feelings and emotions you experience in your belly. Go for it. Have fun with this one! There's usually a lot of feelings and images to work with here.

## Example

*My Belly: Positive and Negative — Anais, 12*

Negative: Rotting bad food
   *Positive: Positive is eating up all negativity*
Negative: Closing in and out with my nervousness
   *Positive: Dancing its feelings out*
Negative: Not being able to eat sugar, grains, or dairy
   *Positive: Why I am small*
Negative: Cramps grow stronger and stronger by the second
   *Positive: What a gift to be alive*

Negative: My bloated stomach is as large as a rainbow lollipop
  *Positive: My stomach is as oval as a lychee fruit*
Negative: Screaming *"I am hungry"* when I'm not
  *Positive: I have so many friends like colon, liver,*
  *gallbladder, and pancreas*
Negative: No negativity
  *Positive: Please more positivity*
Negative: But what can I say, there has to be a little
  negativity
  *Positive: Stay in the moment, and stay positive!*

## Body Language

We spend a lot of time telling ourselves how to think and feel about our bodies. But what if we allowed our bodies to speak to us? What stories would they tell?

 INVITATION: If we allowed our body to speak to us, what would it say? Does some part of your body have something to tell to you — a message, a question, a rant, a pearl of wisdom? Let your body speak. What story does it want to tell?

 JUST WRITE! Close your eyes and listen to your body. Does a certain part of your body call your attention? Allow this part to speak. Write down anything and everything it has to say. What does it want you to know? Allow your body to tell you its story.

## Example

*Lips! — Gillian, 18*

Lips!
You succulent little fruits
you tender little creatures
two red crescent moons
meeting in the middle
for a midnight kiss
wiggling and waggling
the whole day long.

Puffed out and pouty
taut and angry
pursed, pissed, and pushy
demanding, persistent, spitting and spatty
won't take no for an answer
won't let you get a word in edgewise.

Or…
Soft and open
wishing, wanting, asking
smiling with joy
smiling with anticipation
smiling like a little devil.

Chewing and cooing
nibbling and nitpicking
smacking and smooching
humming

and singing out loud.
Or, uh-oh…
YELLING!
Then…
Silent and withdrawn
a dam holding back a river of fury
gates locked
closed for business.

Nothing gets in
nothing gets out
retreat into a silence
louder than words.

## Body-Love Poems

*Embrace and love your body.*
*It's the most amazing thing you'll ever own.*
— ANONYMOUS

 **INVITATION:** Now is the time to celebrate your body! Consider your favorite part of your body. What do you love about it? Describe the way it looks, moves, feels, and functions. What is your relationship with this part of your body? Be honest, sassy, bold, silly, seductive.

 **JUST WRITE!** Write a love poem to your favorite body part. Describe it. Celebrate it.

## Example

*What My Tongue Has Seen — Violet, 11*

My tongue had seen the inside of calamari, which my eyes
     have not
If she's lucky, she's seen the tip of my nose

She knows what the backs of my teeth look like
I'm pretty sure only my dentist knows what's back there

She's seen everything I've eaten
And the jelly bean I spit out

My tongue gives me information
On whether that candy is sweet or sour

My tongue has only glimpses of a mirror
She thinks she's enormous

She dreams of closing her senses to that gross chewed-up
     food
And focusing instead on the cheering of her taste buds

Of all the body parts, the tongue is the only one who
     knows taste
But she can also feel and twist and see with her one flabby
     finger

My tongue has played dress-up with ice cream
She has danced with gum

Her gymnastics skills are divine
But she is envious of anteaters

My tongue helps tell stories and jokes
She's seen poems and presentations

She knows what it is to be heard

### • *Dig Deeper* •

Now is the time to write a poem to a part of your body you judge, criticize, ignore, feel shame about, don't ever talk about, or simply have never considered or celebrated, such as but not limited to your hair, hips, thighs, calves, feet, toes, back, arms, chest, breasts, booty, genitals. Be willing to not know what you're going to write until you write it. It's your choice whether to share this poem or keep it to yourself.

## Get Artsy!

Get a roll of recycled art paper or tape together a bunch of paper bags and have a friend trace your body. The tracing doesn't need to be perfect, just a rough outline of your body shape. Write your body poems inside and outside the outline of your body. Write love poems to your body, write from the different voices of your body parts. Do you see a theme emerging? Use colored markers. Draw and decorate. Color yourself beautiful, wise, wonderful, weird. Have a blast!

## Three Secrets of Sex

Our teen years are usually when our sexuality begins to bloom. We are bubbling with hormones, sexual feelings, and a new curiosity about others, and it can be both exciting and confusing; it sure was for me. It can feel like we're entering uncharted wilderness, and in a sense, we are. How do we reconcile our instinct and our intellect? How do we make wise choices? Where and to whom do we turn for guidance to help us navigate our way? We can easily get lost and hurt in the sexual wilderness, or we can learn to trust ourselves, track our choices, be true to ourselves, communicate clearly and openly, and make sex and sexual feelings a healthy and fulfilling part of our lives.

Some people are born knowing exactly who they are and what they want sexually, while others need time to explore and experiment. Your way is the right way. Your sexual orientation, gender identity, and relationship style are your choice. What matters is that you are in integrity with yourself and others. Voiced consent and safe-sex practices are essential on the part of everyone involved.

As we mature, sex becomes integral to our lives and our relationships, and yet there's this nonverbal agreement that we don't discuss it. It is, after all, how we all got here! When my parents told me about the birds and the bees, they basically boiled it down to: *This is how we make babies.* They never mentioned that it feels good, or that I might like it, or that the experience could bring me into deeper connection with myself and my partner. My mother never even talked to me about my clitoris. That's like telling me how to make ice cream but not mentioning that it's delicious. How is this possible?!

I believe our capacity for wise choices, greater fulfillment, and wholeness as human beings necessitates open discussion about sex, whether within the privacy of our poetry, in our intimate relationships, or in the larger context of our communities. I will share a few secrets that I've learned over the years. Take what works for you, ditch what doesn't, and do your own safe and healthy research to learn what's true for you.

The first secret to sex is...*being (true to) yourself.* Be yourself and be true to who you are. Listen to your body, mind, and heart. You're the only one who knows what is true for you. Trust yourself. If you don't, keep learning until you do. Be careful not to change yourself into what someone else wants. You'll come up unfulfilled. Don't conform or contort in order to fit in and be accepted. You'll never be happy this way. Find out who you are, and accept yourself. Loving yourself, being true to yourself, is the deepest sense of belonging there is. This is your power. Use it!

The second secret to sex is...*communication.* Talking clearly and openly about sex with your partner(s) can create a whole world of trust, intimacy, and fulfillment. There is plenty to discover, experience, and share sexually. Be curious. Ask questions. Practice deep listening. Speak up for yourself. Sex is a shared exploration in which anything goes, as long as you and your partner(s) are in consent. *Yes* is a spectrum, with many shades of what is permissible, to be determined by each person in each new experience. And *No* is a complete sentence that needs to be respected.

The third secret to sex is...*beginner's mind.* In Zen the term *beginner's mind* refers to approaching something with fresh eyes, experiencing something as though for the first time. So rather than buying into conditioned models of sexuality, we can tune in to our own felt experience, taking our cues from inside rather than outside ourselves, and allowing our beautiful, free, sensual bodies to respond naturally. Approaching sexual connection with this kind of openness invites us to feel, discover, express, and share ourselves fully in our own way. In doing so, we make ourselves at home in the wilderness of our sexuality. The passion, electricity, and nourishment we feel when our sexual energy is flowing can become a potent elixir that feeds our life force, fueling and tuning us into greater depths of aliveness and connection with ourselves and our partner(s).

If you are currently being sexually abused in any way, or if you have at any time in the past, please get help and support. You are not alone. There are effective therapeutic tools available that address and unwind sexual trauma, returning people to wholeness. If you are struggling with gender identity or sexual orientation, please get support. It's important to your survival and well-being.

INVITATION: Think about your relationship with sex, your sexuality, your gender identity. How or from whom did you learn about sex? Whether you're new to sex or more experienced, call to mind your best and worst sexual experiences. What made them good or bad, and why? What did you learn from them? What would you like to do differently next time? Are you able to talk about sex with your partner(s)? Do you feel empowered sexually, as in knowing what you want and being able to ask for it? Do you have any concerns or fantasies you'd like to explore in your writing?

 JUST WRITE! Write about your relationship with sex, sexual orientation, or gender identity. What is your experience of gender? What is your experience of sex? What does sex feel like for you? Write about what you like or don't like about sex. Write about a good or bad sexual experience. What are your sexual concerns, desires, fantasies?

With respect to healthy boundaries, it's your choice whether or not to share your sexual poetry, and with whom. Do what's right for you.

## Examples

*We — Loreli, 19*

your body
your hands
your lips
your breath
your voice
on me
in me
with me

lush
velvet
rapture

you inside
me
me inside
you

no me
no you
We

the (di)vine
on which

We flower.

*He/She/They — Taylor, 16*

I am not to be confined
or defined
or refined
or assigned

I want the biggest container I can find
with secret passageways
hidden doors
magic gardens
that lead to new adventures
each time I journey there

I don't want to be squeezed into a jar
that determines my shape

I don't want a lid
screwed down
or tamped into place

I'd rather be a girl than a boy
as a girl I have so much more space
for self-expression
moods up and down
color and creativity
giggling with girlfriends
and no-man's-land

But I'd rather be a boy than a girl
if I'm a boy, other people don't expect me to live up
to their expectations of beauty and politeness
I am my own authority
I say whatever I want
I make my own choices
I make my own mistakes
I choose my own success

So I choose neither and both
I choose to be a living, breathing human being
where all my colors flow, high and low
where there are no limits
on how I explore, express,
speak, walk, dance, love, dress
I am okay being a mystery.

## · 11 ·

# Message in a Bottle

*Songs for me are like a message in a bottle.*
*You send them out to the world, and maybe the person*
*you feel that way about will hear about it someday.*
— TAYLOR SWIFT, interview for *The Daily Beast*

Inspirational messages can come to us in many forms, from out in the world and from within our own imagination and inner wisdom. If we pay attention to the clues, we get the perfect message we need at the perfect moment. One time I was having a rough morning; I was running late, and then I got caught in traffic. I was very stressed, when suddenly I looked up, and the license plate on the car in front of me said: LOVENOW. I laughed and switched right out of my bad mood. The message reminded me to be here in this moment and make the best of it. Every time I go camping, the dragonflies always lead me to the best spot. So whenever I arrive at an appointment or meeting, and I see a picture of a dragonfly, I know I'm in the right place. It's fun to develop a relationship with the part of our mind that is open to receiving helpful messages.

Do people really send messages in bottles? I've always

loved the idea of a message in a bottle. Have you ever found or sent one? Once on a lark, I corked a few bottles with my poems inside, included my address, and asked if found to return to me with a note. I released the bottles into the San Francisco Bay. As of yet, I have not received any return notes.

 INVITATION: Choose whether to write or receive a message in a bottle. Try both!

 JUST WRITE! If you write a message, what does it say? Is it for anyone in particular? If you receive a message, what does it say? Who is it from? What does it mean for you? Where did you find it? What does the bottle look like? Describe the note. What kind of paper is it written on? Is it handwritten or typed? If handwritten, describe the handwriting.

## Example

*Message in a Bottle — Libby, 19*

An old banged-up bottle
washes up at my feet
as I walk with my head down
along the sandy shore

It's corked, and I pick it up
a slight flutter inside
a tarnished scroll
black scribble

I look around
Is anyone watching?
I pry the cork out in pieces
a musty odor escapes

Scrawled in thick letters
from a fountain pen
Trembling, I read,
I have been waiting for you my whole life!

Me?

I look around again to see if anyone's watching
Not quite sure what to do
I stuff the slip of paper back into the bottle
and toss the bottle back into the surf

## Journal Scrap

As I mentioned in chapter 1, I once lugged around a box of about eighty old journals for twenty years. I couldn't make myself read them, but I couldn't let go of them either. Part of me hoped that someday, after I was dead, someone would find them and read them, and know me better, but eventually it was more important that I read them to know myself. Reading back through my journals helped me to integrate, claim, and make peace with my past. After I read them all, I took them to the dump. But what if someone had found them, and what if, while they were reading through one, a scrap of paper fell out with a note or poem about the very person who was reading the journal?!

INVITATION: Imagine that your parent, grandparent, other family member, or friend has gone away or died and that you're reading through their journal. A scrap of paper falls out onto the floor, and you pick it up and see that it's a note or poem written about you.

 JUST WRITE! Write about what you find written on the scrap of paper. Whose journal is it from? What was your relationship with this person? What does the message mean for you?

## Example

*Who Said So?* — *Alyssa, 14*

Who said so?
Those who believe on the surface
they are right.
Deep down they are wrong.
Rules began from someone's beliefs
and now we must follow them.
But in nature there are no rules.

The rings of the tree's heart
are fully their own.
The true-blue infinite sky
showers the ocean with tears
and shimmers the ruffled waves
to a beat
winding and spinning
like a trail un-journeyed.

Each constellation,
a composition
a masterpiece strung together
a dusting of stars.

They're who says so.

The emerald of the trees who root us down
the trickle of the tiny stream
a blazing fire inside
the dream to reach the base
of the mountain
they have explored.

The natural glow to go
where the path doesn't lead
to swim off with the stream
away from the tide
to sail into the waves
with the wind in my face.

I am free
and only my own.
I say so.

## Fortune Flower

Imagine a magic flower that blooms once every five years. It is blooming today, in a nature area near you. You walk to the spot with your best friend and see the flower opening its petals. You hold out your hands as one of the petals falls into your open palm. It's smooth as satin and it smells like honey. You notice a message written on the petal, just one line, like a fortune from a cookie, a song lyric, or a line from a poem. The message is exactly what you need to hear at this moment.

 INVITATION: Read the message on the petal. It was written just for you. You're about to show your friend, when the petal dissolves in your hand.

 JUST WRITE! What did your fortune say? What does it mean for you?

## Examples

*You Are Not Delicate — Mikayla, 10*

You are not delicate.
You are the moonlight of unique iridescence.
You are nothing but love drifting away on a summer day.
You are like a rough teddy bear nobody wants to cuddle.
You are a dog that got lost in the river and then got found
    by a loving one.
You are a beautiful monster who drifted off to sleep like a baby.
You are a bucket of sequins shining bright.
You are a screw whirling in the wind like a butterfly nobody
    wants to tame.
You are my sunshine.
I see through a mirror not knowing where you are.
You are a bunch of carrots getting sold, getting transferred.

Home by home. Mouth by mouth.
You are safe by my side, like a precious diamond shining
    bright.
You are not delicate.


*A Flower's Journey — Tess, 11*

Where does the sun go when she cries?
A joyous tear falls from the sky
startled from the fall
she plunges deep into the damp soil

Sprouting up
she lets the sweet aroma of the earth consume her
She resembles a mini-sun
shining so radiantly she illuminates all she touches

She looks up and sees a towering maple tree
and she wonders what it would feel like to be so tall
The thought blows her away to a clearing deep in the woods
where she is inspired to grow even higher

But days later, she withers
leaving nothing but a pile of dirt behind her
a gift for the earth

A week later, I find her grave
with this message:
*Beauty never fully leaves your soul.*

## Tattoo

*My body is my journal, and my tattoos are my story.*
— Johnny Depp

So many people have tattoos these days. Getting one has almost become a rite of passage. The other day I heard someone say, "I think I'll be a rebel, and *not* get a tattoo!" If anyone had told me how much it would hurt, I may not have done it, but I understand now that the pain is part of the ritual. When I was thirty, I got a tattoo of an art nouveau dragonfly whose wings span my whole upper back. Its tail is a caduceus, the ancient Greek or Roman symbol for healing. There is a lot of symbolism in the dragonfly for me. Insects are survivors who constantly adapt. Dragonflies are the highest- and fastest-flying insect, and many of them live for only twenty-four hours. In certain Native American mythologies, the dragonfly dispels illusions. Lately I've noticed that a lot of people are getting words, phrases, and mantras tattooed on their bodies to remind them of what's important. If I got one now, it would simply say *Love Now!*

 INVITATION: Imagine you wake up in the morning to find a message tattooed on your forearm, a message that affirms your life in a positive way.

 JUST WRITE! What does the tattoo say? What is the meaning of the message for you? How did it get there? What color is it? What language is it? What

font is it written in? Does it appear all at once or in stages?
How do you apply the message of the tattoo to your life?

## Example

*My Tattoo — Alex, 17*

I wake early on Sunday morning
to find peacock-blue letters
in a scrolling font
winding around my right arm
like a snake
I try to catch it by the tail
but it keeps moving
it's alive
writhing and writing itself
as I watch
it says,
*Say Yes, Say Yes*
over and over
along the length of my arm
then it jumps
winding around my left arm
it writes,
*Say No, Say No*
over and over.
I laugh to myself
this will be a hit
in my martial arts class
when I punch, *Say Yes, Say Yes*

when I block, *Say No, Say No*
I cross my arms over my chest
watching the snakes of letters intertwine
knowing both these phrases
are equally important.

## • 12 •

# No Trespassing

*I sat with my anger long enough*
*until she told me her real name was grief.*
— ISAAC ROWE, *I Love Anger*

In this culture, we are taught early on that certain feelings are okay and others are not. Boys don't cry. Girls don't express anger. Shame is something we never talk about. Stuff your guilt. Only wimps are afraid. You're a bad person if you feel desire. If you're sad or depressed, get over it. This kind of thinking cuts us off from knowing what we really feel and from experiencing the range of emotions that make us whole and human. Our feelings are a rich resource; they make us who we are and give us important information about what's happening in our lives. But so many of us are taught to push our feelings away, hide and stuff them inside, until they explode in some way that is harmful to ourselves and others. In my family, depression was allowed but anger wasn't. So I spent a lot of my life depressed. I had a therapist who told me depression is hurt turned inward on ourselves and anger is hurt turned outward toward the world. When I first learned how to be angry, it felt like an accomplishment. I celebrated my anger. It felt healthy to stop turning it into depression and powerlessness and instead to address what I was feeling. I found that my hurt and anger usually come from a need not being met. If I can get to the core of the need, I can address it and ask for what I need. Let's take our hidden and stuffed feelings out and give them a place to speak and be heard. They are our allies. They have wisdom to offer us. You'll be amazed at how much more energy you have when you get in touch with what you really feel, want, and need. Writing helps us metabolize what we keep inside, feeding us with the information we need to grow.

 INVITATION: Think about which emotions you've been told are acceptable and which ones you've been told are not. Look inside yourself and see if there are certain feelings you do, and do not, allow yourself. How would it feel to give yourself permission to experience all your feelings, especially the ones you usually push away or block? The most common feelings we run from are shame, guilt, fear, anger, grief, and desire. Are there any others for you? Perhaps you even push away your joy. Let's look inside.

JUST WRITE! One at a time, touch into each of these feelings: shame, guilt, fear, anger, grief, and desire. How easy or difficult is it for you to access these feelings? Which do you allow or block in yourself? Are there other feelings you've been taught are wrong? Sadness, perhaps? Spend some time with each feeling, sit with it, give it your attention. Listen in to it, allow it to have a voice, shape, texture, temperature, or color. Write from the voice or sensation of each feeling. What does it want or need to say? Is there anything it wants you to hear and know? How does it feel to allow these feelings to be alive in you?

## Examples

*Shame — Kara, 17*

I like boys
I like girls
I didn't know you weren't supposed to
I didn't know I'd show up at school
to see my name painted
next to the word SLUT
in big red letters
on the gym wall.

*Guilt — Melissa, 15*

I wanted it
so I took it.
No, it wasn't mine
but I didn't care.
   I just wanted it.

It was so pretty
bright and silver
with a big turquoise stone
staring out at me,
   like a peacock's eye.

I've had so many
of my own belongings stolen
money, clothing,
even boyfriends.
        Why can't I steal too?

Because every time I look at that bracelet
my stomach flips and flops
my hands and feet go tingly and numb
I feel like I'm going to pass out.
        I can't even wear it now.

*Fear — Anahera, 15*

Piano blares through the empty silence.
Cluttered notes surround the darkness
enclosing it in chaotic harmony.
How can chaos be so beautiful?

"Just breathe," they say.
But a breath can never change this pounding ache.
A breath can never change this deep resonating
within my bones, encasing my fractured mind
in a buzzing sensation.
Is this what they all call Fear?

It doesn't show its face often.
Somehow it's ashamed of all it can do.
But it shouldn't be ashamed.
Fear is a risk by itself,

defying everything
just to make its way to us.
Fear is wild, but it's true.
Why is it that we fear, Fear?

Before I make a choice, I always
have a moment of doubt, a glimpse of fear,
a slight bitterness that leaves me with a
rough taste in my mouth,
like I've rubbed a rusty nail on my tongue
enough times for its residue to sit there
and breathe.
Maybe Fear fears itself too.

*Hollow Space — Ava, 14*

anger like bite your tongue bloody, grit your teeth, and grin scarier than a frown. wet and soft until you've waded in neck-deep and it closes in, stubborn, sharp. discordant notes too far apart. anger so small and pointy and then you see its shadow envelop you.

fear like hair rising on your neck, sweat cold and shiver chilling your body. hands clasping over the crevice, rocky bottom shrouded in clouds, bits broken as fragile and brittle as you. not the sound of the scream but the silence after. fear burrowing into your ear to whisper doubts you know too well.

guilt like dry lips, opening uneven chapped and closing into a seal of skin. crow pecking for shiny sweet fragments of memory to devour, spit out, make unclean. turning the quiet louder than the noise, drown you in a sea of voices squawking in regret. guilt behind you like a ghost, embracing you in empty depth.

## Rant and Rave

*Poetry is a political act because it involves telling the truth.*
— JUNE JORDAN, interview in *Colorlines*

I bet you've got something you'd be willing to stand up and fight for or against, some social or personal issue you feel strongly about. When we rant and rave, we talk loudly, forcefully, or wildly, with rage, passion, or humor about someone or something we have strong feelings or opinions about. It feels good and healthy to vent, to get something off your chest, fight for a cause you believe in, speak out about something you feel is right or wrong. I had a friend who used to trail-run, and when no one was around, he'd yell out loud about all the things that were bothering him to get them out of his system. He always came back glowing. I had another friend who yelled her anger into the ocean, where no one could hear her. She said it felt good to release it from her body. We can do this on paper too.

 INVITATION: Think about an issue or cause you have strong feelings and opinions about, something you're willing to fight for or against. Think in terms of personal, social, political, and global issues such as, but not limited to, abortion, addiction, affordable housing, ageism, animal rights, artistic freedom, birth control, bullying, capital punishment, cheating, child and social services, climate crisis, creative expression, conservation, corruption, crime, disability rights, discrimination, drugs, environmental issues, education, equal pay, equal rights, euthanasia, freedom of speech, gun control, homelessness, immigrant rights, incarceration and rehabilitation, LGBTQ rights, lying, medical care, physical abuse and fighting, poaching, recycling, religion, sexual harassment, sex trafficking, slavery, teen pregnancy, teen suicide, theft, world hunger.

 JUST WRITE! Write a rant against or a rave for an issue you feel strongly about. Have fun with this. Say everything you've ever wanted to say about this topic. Now is your chance. Rant and rave poems are great to do with a group. They make for strong and lively spoken-word poems. After you write, read your pieces out loud, with conviction. Notice how you feel.

## Example

*Rehabilitation vs. Incarceration — Daniel, 18*

Being locked up is punishment in itself
You miss birthdays and holidays
You don't get to see anyone you care about
You miss out on seeing your siblings grow
All your relationships fall apart
Why not focus on helping incarcerated people to better
    themselves
Teach us how to have a better life when we're released

Teach us skills we can use in the outside world
Help us stay out of trouble
Most of the time we're just learning how to cope with our
    emotions
so we won't be so impulsive
but no one really expects us to be able to get a job with a
    criminal record
Then they wonder why we turn back to crime for money
Teach me a trade
Teach me to be a carpenter, plumber, welder, or electrician
Teach me something I can do to make a living when I'm
    released
so I don't have to return to a life of crime.

## Burn, Baby, Burn

*We all have our secrets. To withhold words is power.*
*But to share our words with others,*
*openly and honestly, is also power.*

— TERRY TEMPEST WILLIAMS, *When Women Were Birds*

There are poems we write that we never want anyone to read, but it sure feels good to finally write them down and give voice to the secrets we hold inside. Getting honest with ourselves is a form of freedom. Honesty is the lightning in a storm. What we bring to light eventually frees us. It's what we hold inside that consumes us and splits us off from ourselves and others. Here is a chance to write what you've been holding inside. I find that writing down secrets transforms the shame, guilt, or negativity into acceptance. Give it a try.

Dig deep. Say the things in this poem that you've never told anyone, the things you can't bear to let others know about you, the secrets you guard with your life. You get to choose whether to keep or burn your poems.

 INVITATION: Read through the statements below, and choose one or two that feel scary. These are the ones you need to write about. Remember, you can burn your poems.

 JUST WRITE! Write about one or two of the statements below that make your heart beat a little faster, make you hold your breath, make you sweat or swallow hard. After you've written your poem, read it to yourself, then choose whether to keep it or burn it.

### • *Burn, Baby, Burn Statements* •

The worst thing I ever did was…

My most embarrassing moment was…

Once I stole…

I'm afraid of…

What I really want to say to my parents, my partner, (or to whomever) is…

I find it hard to talk about…

The thing that really upsets me about this person is…

The secret I've never told anyone is…

I'm jealous of…

I think I might be crazy because…
I have a huge crush on…
My first kiss…
My first sexual experience…
My best sexual experience…
My worst sexual experience…

There are no EXAMPLE poems. We burned them all!

## • 13 •

# Dream Catcher

*At the center of your being you have the answer.*
— M. J. Ryan, *A Grateful Heart*

We live in a society where we are taught to seek direction, answers, and a sense of belonging from the world and people outside of ourselves. Mass culture manipulates us into believing we can fill our deeper needs for connection, intimacy, and purpose with material possessions rather than transformative experiences. Many of us grow up feeling disenchanted, disconnected, disappointed, lost, lonely, empty, and bereft. Often the pain of these feelings is what finally leads us to seek deeper communion with ourselves in order to find our greater purpose, passion, and peace. Let me introduce you to some of my favorite tools for accessing your own inner wisdom.

## Spirit Animal

*I belong to the black cat with fire green eyes.*
*There, in the cypress tree near the morning star.*
— JOY HARJO, *Conflict Resolution for Holy Beings*

Some Native Americans believe that we all have spirit animals who act as our guides, protectors, and teachers whom we can call on for strength, wisdom, and companionship. I have participated in Native American ceremonies in which we journey to a drumbeat to receive healing and wisdom. The sound of the drumbeat creates delta brain wave activity that allows us access to deeper states of consciousness. Before each journey, we meet and create relationships with our power animals so they can protect and aid us on our journey. You never know which animal is going to show up to help you. You may be surprised. Everyone thinks they want a regal animal like an eagle or a cheetah, but many animals you wouldn't consider special can offer great power, skill, strategy, and wisdom. Some of my spirit animals are wolf, fox, monkey, snake, owl, and luna moth. What are yours?

 INVITATION: Meet your spirit animal. Sit comfortably, close your eyes, and take a couple of deep breaths. Clear your mind and ask for your spirit animal to reveal itself to you. Whatever animal shows up, be open and say hello, and ask if it is your helper. Wait for an answer. If it says no, or nothing at all, ask it to leave, and then ask again for your spirit animal to come to you. When your spirit animal shows up, you will feel it. Trust what you feel. When you feel a solid connection of support and protection from the animal, thank it and ask it what message it has for you. Wait until the message is clear. Messages don't always come in words. Sometimes they come in images or feelings or a sense of knowing. Trust whatever message you receive, in whatever form it comes. Ask if you can call on this animal again. You may have more than one spirit animal.

 JUST WRITE! Write about your experience meeting your spirit animal. Review the How to Write about Your Spirit Animal list below. What animal came to you? Describe it. How did you know it was your spirit animal? How did it communicate with you? What qualities do you relate to in this animal? What strengths and characteristics does this animal bring that you can learn from? What message or wisdom does it have for you? What does this animal and its message mean for you?

• *How to Write about Your Spirit Animal* •

My spirit animal is a…
My spirit animal looks like…
I know this is my spirit animal because…
I relate to this animal because…
It communicates with me in this way…
When I'm with this animal, I feel…
What I learn from this animal is…
Its wisdom, strength, or message for me is…

## Examples

*Panther — Jake, 17*

Dark and sleek
you stay close to me like a shadow
sliding along with me in every direction,
we move together as one being.

I fall asleep against your thick, warm fur
and dream of jungles
and beautiful women,
wildflowers in their hair.

Morning rain comes and wakes me.
Birds are singsonging.
My limbs ache to run through grass savannas
chasing giraffe and zebra.

You teach me to walk silently
To hunt effortlessly
To take only what I need
and leave the rest for others.

You mark me with one quick claw,
drawing blood from my shoulder.
Now we belong to each other.
Now we are family.

You travel inside me
and I travel inside you.

I look out at the world through your eyes
and the world is alive!


*Quetzal — Willa, 12*

Singing voices of the trees
Warm sun reflecting off the water by the falls
Turquoise quetzal bird
floats down to the water's edge.

A low tune drifts along the tips of its wings
as it hops onto my arm.
Every color of the rainbow
is drizzled onto its shimmering feathers.

The wispy tail feathers
make my skin feel calm and happy
as it whispers to me,
    "Never do what anyone tells you
        when you know it's wrong."


## Inner Shaman

Among indigenous cultures worldwide, the shaman, or "wise one," is a healer. Shamanism is an ancient healing tradition, a way of living connected with all of nature and life. Shamans believe in animism, that everything is alive and that every-thing, including objects, has a spirit or energy. Shamans take a holistic view of a person and see them as connected to self, community, nature, and all of life. They believe that if you're sick, a corresponding part in your thoughts, emotions, actions, or relationships is out of balance. They view disease as a disconnection or an imbalance in the weave of the fabric of the web of life.

As dancer and writer Gabrielle Roth said, "In many shamanic societies, if you came to a medicine person complaining of being disheartened, dispirited, or depressed, they would ask one of four questions: 'When did you stop dancing? When did you stop singing? When did you stop being enchanted by stories? When did you stop being comforted by the sweet territory of silence?'"

All shamans have suffered a major life event that challenged and changed them, bringing them close to death and giving them access to the spirit world. If they survive, they return to the tribe with wisdom and power they use to help others. I think all poets are shamans. We write our way through our darkness and disconnection with self and community, and we write our way back, returning with something to share, a map, a remedy, a way of wisdom.

 INVITATION: Meet the shaman, or wise one, who resides within you and to whom you can go anytime for strength, support, and wisdom. Who is your inner shaman? What would you like to ask them? What question or issue do you want support with? You may have more than one. You may have a whole team of wise people who you can sit with in counsel.

Over many years of my doing shamanic journey work to a drumbeat, I have made contact with a few members of my inner council. One of my shamans is Cypress, an elder who is 130 years old. She is strong and agile, her eyes are clear and lively, but her face and hands are deeply weathered. She has white hair down to her ankles, and she comes to me in a small rowboat at the edge of a riverbank. She invites me to sit in her boat, and the gentle rocking of the boat relaxes me. She takes my hand, looks into my eyes with compassion and curiosity, and listens as I ask for her help: *What should I do next in my life, how do I handle the problem in this relationship, what choice do I make about this or that?* She answers with kindness and clarity. Her answers always ring true. After consulting with her, I know what to do. I thank her. Before I leave, she always puts something she has made into my hands, a piece of brightly woven cloth or a beaded bracelet, a treasure she has found, like an owl feather or a deer antler. In this way she is always with me.

Close your eyes and take a couple of deep breaths, clear your mind, and ask your inner shaman to come out and meet you. Be curious. Who shows up? When someone appears, check in with what you feel. You should feel safe and supported in their presence. Ask if they are there to help you. If they say yes, thank them, and ask your question. Listen for the answer. It doesn't always come in words. Sometimes it comes in a feeling or an image. Be open and receptive to how your inner shaman communicates with you.

 **JUST WRITE!** Write about your experience. Who showed up as your inner shaman? Were you surprised? What did they look like? Describe them in detail. What question did you ask? What answer did you receive? How did they communicate with you? How do you apply this answer to your life?

## Example

*The Wise One — Mercedes, 19*

She's tall and lean
a long braid down her back
her skin tanned and taut.
Are you my inner guide?
No, she says. I am your sister.
I will bring you to the Wise One, come.
We ride a Bengal tiger
up through the clouds to a high mountaintop
where a tiny cottage sits nestled in a cave.
I walk inside.
It's warm and lit by firelight.
An old woman sits at a table
pouring tea like she expects me.
I sit across from her and she takes my hand.
What can I do for you? she asks.
Will I ever find true love?
Yes, she says, as soon as you fully love yourself.
When you love yourself you are irresistible.
I take a deep breath. I know this is true.
So, how do you feel about yourself?
she asks, her eyes bright and playful.
Pretty damn good, I say.
You should, she says.
She presses a small stone into my palm
and says, *Believe in yourself.*
I feel the stone grow warm and hum.
I thank her and turn to go.
Who are you? I ask.

*I am you, just older*, she says.
*And you are me, just younger.*
She winks at me
and I leave feeling strong and confident.

## Dream Catcher

*In dreams we enter a world that is entirely our own.*
— ALBUS DUMBLEDORE,
in *Harry Potter and the Prisoner of Azkaban*, J. K. Rowling

Do you remember your dreams? When I was a child, I remembered all my dreams, and I wrote them down every morning. I had a pile of notebooks filled with dream descriptions. Once every few years I would read back through them, and I could see patterns, things I struggled with. It didn't matter what forms they took in my dreams; the feelings were clear, and I had a sense of what they symbolized. I tracked each dream symbol as I confronted it, eventually made peace with it, and witnessed it slowly dissolve. Dreams are a bridge into our deep psyche. They are our subconscious mind sorting the material of our lives. Our dreams can give us helpful insights and information, even creative ideas and practical solutions to real-life problems. But they can also be unsettling and downright scary at times. The worst thing is waking up in the middle of the night from a scary dream, shaken, not knowing how it ends and not wanting to go back to sleep and risk entering the dream again. There is a Native American approach to working with nightmares and disturbing dreams: catch the dream before it fades and invent or change the ending!

INVITATION: Choose a recent or recurring dream you have had, one with an unsettling or scary ending. Or choose one that leaves you hanging when you wake up in the middle of it. Catch the dream before it fades, and get ready.

 JUST WRITE! Write about what you remember from your dream, watching it as if it's a movie you are part of. Now comes the creative work: invent or change the ending to something more positive! See if you can understand the message of your dream.

## Example

*Trust — Stephen, 18*

I am on an island vacation in a convertible sports car. I run out of gas, so I leave my car to go find help, but when I return, my car is gone. I'm stranded without money or belongings. I wake up feeling shaken and angry.

I close my eyes, and a story starts playing like a movie. I'm standing on the side of the road wondering what the hell happened to my car, when a family drives up in my little car. They are smiling and my car is brimming with colorful vegetables.

They tell me their daughter was very sick. They saw the car and they jumped in without thinking and drove to get help for her. Later they realized what they had done. So they came to return the car and filled it with vegetables from their garden to say thank you.

They invite me to their home to share a feast and meet their daughter, who I fall madly in love with. I spend a whole week with them. They feel like family. In this dream I learn how to trust. I learn that even the worst situations can turn out good.

## • Dig Deeper •

Write from the voice of a scary dream character or the scared part of yourself in the dream. Let it speak its truth, without censoring it. See what it wants to say. What is its message for you? Write a conversation between two characters in the dream. Find a way to get them to resolve their differences. What can you learn from their conversation? Are there areas in your waking life where you can apply what you learned?

## Treasure Box

*Someone I loved once gave me a box full of darkness.*
*It took me years to understand that this, too, was a gift.*
— MARY OLIVER, "The Uses of Sorrow"

If you had a secret box containing something that could give you exactly what you need each day to help you be and do your very best, what would it be? Most of the time, the things we really need to make our lives work are qualities we already possess but that we keep just out of our own awareness. As we learn to trust and believe in ourselves, we find we have exactly what we need to meet all our dreams and goals. We just have to look inside and know we are worthy.

 **INVITATION**: Find, make, or imagine a small, magical box. Inside this box is a gift for you. Whatever the box contains will help you lead the life you want. Discover what treasure your box holds. Some treasures my students have discovered include silence, trust, forgiveness, a mirror that always makes them feel beautiful, patience, self-love, self-worth, power, a best friend, wisdom, kindness, gratitude, understanding, even unlimited pizza!

 **JUST WRITE!** Walk into your room and find your treasure box. What does the box look like? Open the box and write about what you find inside.

## Example

*Love — Olivia, 15*

I put my hand in the treasure box
and it sinks right in
a cool squishy suction
that molds around my hand
filling every crevice.

It holds me and feeds me.
It warms me in the center
where the darkness lives
where the loneliness cries.

It plays the harp
sings me to sleep
in a purple flannel womb
with feather pillows
and heating-pad walls
this private velvet chamber.

I am safe here
while fear stalks me in the night
a cat burglar dressed in black rags
his face obscured with cracking paint
the symbols of his war against himself.

## Magic Amulet

There is magic in heirlooms, things that get passed down from generation to generation. There is power in objects and pieces of jewelry that hold meaning for us. Imagine you receive a magic amulet, like a locket, a pocket watch, a compass, or a jewel, from your mother or father. (Or you can write about a real object in your life that has been passed down to you.) It has been in your family for many generations, and now it's yours. The giver hints that it contains some kind of magic, and you have to figure out what it is.

 INVITATION: Sit with the amulet you've just received. What does it look like? What does it feel like in your hand? What is its magic? Open it and find a photo or engraving inside or on the back of it. What do you see?

**JUST WRITE!** Describe your amulet. Is there a picture or engraving somewhere on it, and if so, whose picture is it, or what does it say? If you like, you can choose to put a picture of your choice inside. Whose picture would you choose to put in it? What is the magic of this amulet, and how do you use it?

## Example

*Magic Locket — Malia, 15*

It's small and gold
and definitely old
covered in etchings of curlicue wings.
It's worn smooth in places
like somebody rubbed it
between their fingers.

I look inside
and my great-grandparents
look back at me from sepia-toned eyes.
Who are you, little apple?
they ask me.

I rub the locket between my thumb and finger.
It shivers and hums.
It opens and asks in a tiny golden voice,
What shall we do today?

Wondering if I've gone crazy
I try to grab it and shut it
but it flies into the air,
flapping each of its golden wings.
Come on, it flutters, let's go!
Where? I ask.
Anywhere you want, it says,
laughing in a voice made of bells and birdsongs.

But I don't know where I want to go.
I don't know what I want to do.
I hang my head and kick the dirt
and stuff it back into my pocket.

Where are you happiest?
it squeaks from inside my pocket.
I think about a day at the beach last summer
and how happy I was, in the sunshine
running through the water
dancing across the sand.

We're going to the beach! It sings
as it breaks free from my pocket
flying in circles like a drunk butterfly.
Do what you love! it whispers,
in a voice made of sunset and dreams.

## Open the Door

*In the universe, there are things that are known and things*
*that are unknown, and in between, there are doors.*

— WILLIAM BLAKE, *Songs of Innocence and Experience*

Think of a door as a metaphor for choice, opportunity, possibility. A door is an entrance or an exit. A space between. A way to move out of one place and into another. Imagine a door in front of you. Open it, and discover what comes next in your life!

 **INVITATION:** Think about what door, symbolically, you need or want to go through at this moment in your life. What's on the other side of a door that could help you? Is anything holding you back from opening this door?

 **JUST WRITE!** Close your eyes and imagine a door. What does it look like? Imagine opening this door into a new life in which you feel happy and fulfilled. Open the door!

### Example

*Many Doors — Kylie, 16*

A metallic glass door with a wavy pattern on the side.
Running my hand over the surface
and recognizing height charts from when I was a child.

Careful words and rash ones are stored here.
I turn the handle and open the door.

Another door behind it, exactly as before, only now a little
    larger.
The writing on it is etched deeper, darker, and far more
    clear.
"Things I must overcome," the door says.
All over the surface are etched my faults.
My temper, my ego, my stubbornness,
they look to have been carved with a belt knife
as easily as if the glass was soft wood.

I open the second door. "Things I must accept."
The list is longer than before.
There is more room, for the door has doubled in size.
I open it again. "Things I must apologize for."

I open this door quickly and absentmindedly.
"Things I have wanted to say." This is a little out of place.
I scan it and realize that this shouldn't be here for everyone
    to see.
I shatter it with a conveniently located baseball bat.

"Things I must confess." This one stops me cold.
Reading along the first of a thousand entries, I open this
    one as well.
"Things I must do." I start to open it and stop.
I can't. I still have too many things to accomplish.
I shrug and go home, leaving the metallic glass where it stood.

# • 14 •

# We Are Nature

*We often forget that WE ARE NATURE.*
*Nature is not something separate from us.*
*So when we say that we have lost our connection to nature,*
*we've lost our connection to ourselves.*

— ANDY GOLDSWORTHY

Being in nature is the best way I know to connect with myself. From nature, I learn how to be human. For many indigenous cultures, the natural world is the teacher and our connection with nature determines the quality of our connection with ourselves, others, and all of life. My whole life, nature has been my refuge and my temple where I go to remember who I am. Every morning I go for a hike, immersing myself in the natural world and communing with what's inside me and out. During my twenties and thirties, I spent fifteen summers solo backpacking and vision questing, through every national park in the western United States. All summer I backpacked by myself through the wilderness for weeks at a time, hiking, fasting, and meditating. I wanted to dissolve the layers of conditioning that shaped me before I knew I had a choice. I wanted to discover who I truly was, why I was here, what mattered to me, and what I really needed to survive and be happy. I wanted to experience what I called my essence, the deepest part of myself. And once I had a sense of it, touched and tasted it, I wanted to help others know themselves more deeply. I learned a lot about myself during my summer sojourns. I learned how to be alone, how to rely on myself and be resourceful. I learned that I am connected to the whole web of life. I learned that I prefer to live simply, in tune with the cycles of nature and my own tides of ebb and flow, that having enough is plenty for me, and that the source of my happiness is within me. If you've never done a nature retreat or a vision quest, I recommend it, though I suggest going with a friend or group. I still love to spend extended time alone in nature, off grid, but if it's not something you have experience with, try it first with a buddy. I love living outdoors. I spend my summers camping and writing at the Yuba River in Northern California, or soaking in the hot springs in Big Sur, or kayaking with whales in Baja, or swimming with wild dolphins in Hawaii. Most of the year I sleep with the doors of my cottage wide open, to the sounds and smells, to the fresh air. By mid-December it's chilly, but even then, I sleep with my window open. I have grown accustomed to falling asleep to cricket song and waking to morning birds.

## Cycle of Seasons

Let's journey together through the cycle of seasons, within and without, to see ourselves in the mirror of nature and to access a terrain rich in transformation and treasure. The cycle of seasons offers an abundant palette for poetry. All around us, nature's seasons are changing throughout the year, and within us we also experience seasons. Inner seasons are the cycles of birth and growth, death and transformation, that are natural to all life. Our inner seasons provide metaphors for and insight into the life lessons we are journeying through. And just because it's one season outside doesn't mean it's the same season inside us. For example, right now it's winter where I live, but I have so much energy and so many ideas that it feels like I'm in the middle of my very own springtime. Or it could be summer where I live, but I'm so exhausted I can barely move, and that tells me that I'm in a winter cycle; so I'll rest, allow my roots to burrow deep for nutrients and rejuvenation, and see what treasures are there for me. Personal soul seasons can change and shift day to day and week to week, and I've learned to welcome each season with curiosity and acceptance. While my favorite season is summer, I pay close attention to all the seasons, and I find that each is juicy with information and gifts to help me navigate my own cycles. You get to figure out which season you are currently journeying through, what each season's lessons and gifts are for you, and what it means for you at this point in your life. The insights we gain from each season change as we age and grow. Below are examples of how I experience each soul season. Allow my suggestions to inform you, but feel free to come up with your own. It can be fun to revisit this invitation at the beginning of each new season.

## Soul Seasons

**Winter** is the cycle to go within, into the fertile darkness. It is a time of stillness and renewal, when you allow yourself to cease all the doingness and give yourself the gift of beingness. Get warm and cozy. Rest and sleep. Allow your roots to effortlessly extend into the dark earth and feed from the soil of your deep self. As you let go, it can feel like a death, but it is in this in-between space, this dreamtime, where you become part of the mystery of life. Here the seeds for everything new do their own deep work of becoming.

**Spring** is the cycle to burst open like a seed, with new life and new ideas. Everything is possible. Life is hatching and blossoming all around you and within you. Join the chorus of voices reaching up for the warmth of the sun. Cross-pollinate your ideas with the ideas of others, and watch them grow. Springtime is the energy of a child, full of life, love, and promise; it is energy in motion. Wake up. Rise and stretch. Greet the day with curiosity after the long winter. It's time to connect and play!

**Summer** is the cycle to expand and express. Get out and explore. Engage all the ripe and delicious energy of springtime, and share it with others in creative expression and communion with nature. Take advantage of the long summer days and warm summer nights. Grab your friends. Travel. Go camping. Stargaze. Moon-bathe. Immerse yourself in the mystical beauty of sunrise and sunset. Make up songs and poems. Dance and paint. Hike and swim. Pick wild blackberries, and eat them until your fingers and tongue are stained purple. Remember, you are alive!

**Autumn** is the cycle to harvest, a time to reap the treasures from your year. Go for a long walk. Reflect, gather, and honor what you've learned and how you've grown. Acknowledge all you've created and contributed. Gather with community. Share your fruits, and let your labors of love nourish you and others during this time of culmination and celebration before returning to the dark mystery of winter.

 INVITATION: Take a moment and tune in with yourself. Feel the quality of your energy. Think about what soul season you are currently experiencing. Is this a sleepy, slowdown winter dreamtime? Are you just waking and hatching into the springtime of a new you? Are you in the middle of summer, full of sunshine energy? Is it time to reap and share your autumn harvest?

 JUST WRITE! Write about which season your soul is journeying through. What feelings and thoughts are you experiencing in this particular soul season? What are you learning about yourself and your cycles? Try using nature metaphors and similes such as: my heart is on fire like the sun, my body is as slow as mud, my ideas are blooming like wildflowers. Look for the opportunities, lessons, insights, and gifts of your soul season. Write it!

## Example

*Winter — Mikayla, 11*

Winter is a cycle of sadness
where everyone takes their own path of darkness
and feels every moment of this season.

Even the stars start to dim,
and the sun shares its last ray of joy.

The ode of the blackberry is so dark
that not even a single animal can eat its soul.

The loneliness of Winter
is like the happiness of Spring
except kind of the opposite.

I feel like the inside of an apple, soft and hard.
The flowers inside of me close in the Winter.
Every morning I wake up like a sloth,
slow and hungry.
Winter is a cycle.

## Walking Poems

*I took a walk in the woods and came out taller than the trees.*
— ATTRIBUTED TO HENRY DAVID THOREAU

I am one of those people who needs to move my body every day, or I go bonkers. Can you relate? I hike, swim, bike, and dance, but walking, walking, is my meditation. I cannot say enough good things about walking. I have gone for a long walk every day of my life since I was about nine years old. Walking is how I do my best thinking and my best unthinking. When I am walking, the natural cadence of my steps and breath recalibrates my brain and body. Walking makes me feel deeply alive and rejuvenated. No matter what state of mind I'm in, a walk is always the right medicine. When I walk, I find it easy to let go of my mind chatter and simply be present. One thing I love to do while walking is work on a poem. I can take the skeleton of a poem with me on a walk, and by the time I get home, I have it fleshed out to the rhythm of my stride. I can even take a problem out for a walk, and by the time I get home, I know how to handle it. Sometimes I have no idea what I want to do with a poem I'm writing or a workshop I'm teaching, and the minute I put my body in motion, literally ten steps into a walk, I suddenly have the whole picture; I know exactly what I want to do and how to do it. Trust your muse. When was the last time you went for a walk? Let's go!

 INVITATION: Go for a walk outside, in the rain, snow, or sunshine; take a walk at night. Open your senses. Take in everything. Feel the movement of your body. Sense your heartbeat and breath. Find the rhythm of your stride. Let your body guide you. Allow yourself to let go of your mind and your thoughts and just be present with the natural rhythm of your walking. Try taking a poem with you and working on it while you walk, saying the lines to yourself, turning them over and over in your mouth until you find their rhythm and they fit together as seamlessly as your stride.

 JUST WRITE! Choose five things you notice on your walk: images, feelings, and other sensory information. Write a poem weaving these elements together. Allow the rhythm of your strides, your heartbeat, and your breath to inform your poem.

## Example

*Walking in the Desert — Miranda, 18*

The desert floor cracked
under my feet
as I jumped
from cactus bloom
to cactus bloom.
The air wavered in sheets
of cellophane.
My thirst bore a hole in my head
like a sword of focus
pointing me toward
a tilting horizon.
I lost track of time.
My feet blistered and peeled.
I swallowed the sun.
My skin melted.
I drank it like milk.
I surrendered my thorns and needles.
I rolled in the cracked clay
until I shone.

## Nature Treasure

Some of my favorite treasures are objects I've found in nature. Once when I was walking in the surf along the Strait of Juan de Fuca on the Olympic Peninsula in Washington State, I found the scapula of a small creature, smooth and ocean tumbled. I love to look at how the light comes through the thinnest places of the bone. Lately, collecting birds' nests and snakeskins has been my passion. Finding feathers, from red-tailed hawk, wild turkey, owl, is always special. Driftwood makes great sculptures. Stones of serpentine and quartz become jewels in my garden. Some treasures ask that we take them home with us, while others request that we return them to where we found them. It's your call. Follow your intuition.

 INVITATION: Go outside! Take a walk in nature. Pay attention to anything that catches your eye. Pick up a rock, a dried flower, a feather, a piece of driftwood. Sit with your found object and let it speak to you. Where was it born? Hold old is it? How did it get here? What kind of life did it have? What is its wisdom? What does it symbolize for you? What message and power does it offer you?

 JUST WRITE! Write about your treasure. How and where did you find it? What is special about it? What does it teach you about yourself and the world? Do you take it home with you, or do you put it back where you found it?

## Examples

*Feather — Emi, 12*

I am a part of something big
but I can do an amazing thing by myself
I am a feather

I was part of a cormorant
I soared through the sky with the greatest of ease
I dove through the water like a slimy seal

My other parts started to fall until I was the last
I clung on as hard as I could, but finally, I had to let go

I fell to the water and drifted for days
until the sound of waves woke me
I was on a sea of sand

A person picked me up against my cries
He carried me to a room with a desk and papers

He sat down and opened a jar of black goop
He threw me in and pulled me across the paper
making me dizzy like on a roller-coaster ride

Soon after, he left, and I heard glass break
A person with long brown hair came in
and stole me from the desk

She threw me in a bag
and we ran out the window
We went down a ladder
and the wind lifted me up and out of the bag
I was ready for a new adventure.

### Santa Barbara Stone — Marley, 12

I was born on the Santa Barbara beach at the end of July.
I washed up on the shore, bringing my seashell friend with
   me.
He has made himself at home, as part of me.

The holes on my outside have cut deeply into me
after all I have gone through in the ocean.
I've been tossed around by seals.

I've been alive so long that I have been trampled by
   dinosaurs
which is what caused me to flatten
and my holes were stabbed into me by the daggers of their
   rough claws.

But during all I've been through,
my shell friend has helped me.
His kindness is what keeps me soft inside and out.

"That's a beautiful story,"
I say to my new nature friend.
"The shell really did shape your personality well."

Then I take him into my hand
and hold him in my tightly clenched fist
pressing him against my chest.

## Moon Medicine

When was the last time you walked outside at night, looked up, and felt inspired by the moon's beauty? One of the many things I love about the moon is that she's always changing, waxing or waning on her cyclic journey as she circles in the sky, orbiting the earth. She gives me permission to cycle too. To know that sometimes I'm full of energy, and sometimes I'm empty. Sometimes I'm bright and other times dark. Whatever phase I'm going through is welcome; it's part of my journey. Some people feel the pull of the moon on their mood. Often during a full moon, I have crazy creative energy and I stay up all night writing poems or playing my guitar, while on other full moons all I can do is sleep and sleep. Are you influenced by the moon? Does your energy wax or wane in sync with the moon's phases?

The moon is muse to many. Medicine to others. Grandmother Moon to many Native Americans. Moon mythology and ceremony are integral to every culture on earth, especially those of the indigenous peoples. The moon generates the tides with its gravitational pull. The twenty-eight-day moon cycle correlates to women's menstruation cycles. Many women ovulate on the full moon and bleed on the new moon. New moon is often seen as a time to start a project, whereas full moon is the harvest time when we reap what we've sown during the past month's cycle. What about the dark side of the moon? People used to fear the dark shadow side, equating it with the unconscious, the blind spot in which repressed aspects of ourselves are hidden from us. Some say the shadow side is where our secret gardens of taboo grow. Sounds like wild territory to me; let's go! Let's sniff out the metaphor on the shadow side.

I invite you to consider the dark side of the moon and the dark phase of your own cycle as a time of deep connection with yourself, a time when you slow down and listen inside. A time to draw replenishment from rest, quietude, and solitude, and to allow beingness rather than doingness. In my experience, we need both sides of our nature in order to be whole, or we burn out. I believe it is in this dark phase of the moon and our personal dark cycle that we let go of our shape, surrender to a state of goo like the caterpillar, and from this fertile darkness, emerge anew with dark and beautiful wings, glistening with the wisdom and power of our wholeness.

 INVITATION: Go outside and look up at the moon tonight. What phase is she in? Is she waxing or waning? Draw inspiration from the glow, shape, direction, and color of the moon. Consider how the moon's cycles of waxing and waning possibly influence your own cycles of light and dark, fullness and emptiness.

 JUST WRITE! Write about your connection with the moon. Are you aware of any influence it has on your energy? Are you in sync with the cycles of the moon? Do you feel wild and full of life on the full moon or drained and empty? Does the new moon inspire a new project? Write about moon medicine and what it heals in you and others. Write about the song or story you imagine hearing from the moon. Write about how the moon inspires you and helps you to feel connected to the wonder of life as you walk home at night, the moonlight silvering your skin.

## Examples

### *Moonlight — Lila, 11*

Always keep a moonflower near
wear it on a golden chain
and you'll be safe forever.
Touch its sparkling silver petals
and you'll never be sick again.
Make some moonflower tea
mix in a spoonful of stardust
and you'll never be lonely.
Make a moon charm
from moonlight sparkles.
Keep it in your pocket
use it as a wishing stone
and watch all your dreams come true.
Listen to the stories the moon tells
keep them safe
wear them on a charm bracelet
and you'll surely be happy forever.

### *Dark Side — Lila, 11*

I have been to the dark side of the moon
chasing the idea of something unattainable
something smoky
something dark
something that sings an eerie song
unlike anything you have ever heard before.

I have been to the dark side of the moon
chasing a memory I want to forget
chasing the thought of nothing and everything
I have been to the dark side of the moon.

## Mandalas and Talismans

*Everything is ceremony in the wild garden of childhood.*
— PABLO NERUDA, "The Lost Ones of the Forest"

I love to construct art out of natural objects I find. Choose an afternoon to spend outdoors with friends. Collect nature objects to make art: mandalas, or circular wheels of focus, and talismans, or power objects. In my Write of Passage nature program, I dedicate a whole day to this activity. First we collect a bag full of nature treasures, then we build circular mandalas on the beach with the objects we've collected. In these mandalas we put all the limiting thoughts and feelings that we're ready to let go of, such as fear, self-doubt, self-criticism, self-pity, apathy, confusion, you name it, all the things that hold us back. We assemble the mandalas where the tide will come and wash them away, taking all our limiting beliefs with it. Next we build talismans with our remaining nature treasures, tying them to handheld, arm-length branches or pieces of driftwood. We imbue our talisman with all the qualities we want to call into our lives, such as confidence, inspiration, love, compassion, productivity, friendship, creativity, insight, self-worth. We take our talismans home with us to help us remember and call on the power of our intentions we seeded within them. Let's make our own!

INVITATION: You'll need a bag and some twine. Go into nature with a few friends, and walk in silence as you collect a bag full of nature objects, such as branches, seedpods, dried flowers, feathers, rocks, sticks, shells, bones, birds' nests. Think about what these objects symbolize for you. Think about what draining qualities you're ready to let go of in yourself and what qualities you want to call in to empower you. Use your senses when choosing and gathering. Which plants and flowers, alive or dead, call to you? Notice color, texture, symbolism. A bright-green leafy sprig may signify life force, a bird's nest may symbolize home, driftwood could represent resiliency, the ability to tumble through the waves and bob to the surface. Trust your intuition. Whatever you write is right!

**Mandala:** Find a flat spot on the beach or ground. Think about what you're ready to let go of in yourself, what thoughts, feelings, and behaviors no longer serve you. Use about half the objects you've collected. Choose treasures to represent each limiting belief that you're ready to let go of. Arrange your treasures in a circle mandala, like a flower, wheel, or spiral.

 JUST WRITE! When you feel complete with what you've made, write a poem about your experience. How did you choose each piece? What message, magic, or medicine does it hold for you? How does naming this quality, and having something tangible to represent it, help you to see, understand, heal, release, and grow at this moment in your life? After you've written your poem, step away and allow the tide to claim it, the wind to blow it, or the animals, people, and elements to scatter it. Let it go!

**Talisman:** Now take your remaining treasures and find a branch, a large twig, or a piece of driftwood about the length or your hand or lower arm. Think about which qualities you want to call in to empower yourself at this moment in your life, ones to help you respect and value yourself, to trust and believe in yourself, to be true to yourself, and to express yourself fully. Choose pieces from your nature treasures that represent each quality you want to call in. Using your twine, attach these pieces to your branch or driftwood by wrapping the twine around them to bind them to the branch. Feel the power of the talisman you've created, filled with the positive intentions and visions of who you want to become.

 JUST WRITE! When you feel complete with making your talisman, write about your experience. How did you choose the pieces to represent the different qualities? What is the meaning, magic, and medicine of the nature treasures you've chosen? How does it feel to hold this talisman in your hands? Take your talisman home with you. Look at it and hold it when you need to remember your strength, courage, value, and vision.

## Example

*Treasure Maps — Owen, 16*

All morning I walk along the trail
gathering nature skeletons
shells, dried flowers, driftwood

I empty my pockets of self-doubt and loathing
I assemble my treasures
into spiral galaxies on the beach
aligning them with my own constellations
and lunar eclipse

When the tide roars up on the beach
it takes away all the broken pieces of me
I wash myself in the sea
shedding the stench of self-pity
from my skin

I roll on the sand
happy as a dog
light as a bird

I am a tall warrior
I build a home of driftwood and kelp
I am strong and powerful

I make a sword of dreams
I am worthy of love.

# • 15 •

# Write of Passage

*And it was at that age...Poetry arrived
in search of me.*
— Pablo Neruda, "Poetry"

Those of us who find writing as our path develop a deep
and intimate relationship with this medium of self-
discovery and self-expression. Writing becomes a companion. Some people feel writing chooses us. I believe this. As a
kid, when I was disenchanted with society and people, which
was often, I climbed into my own world, where everything
was alive and magical, and I wrote in order to connect with
it. I felt powerful when I wrote things down. I started writing
short stories when I was about five years old, stories about
characters who lived inside me. I sat for hours and hours
by myself in the basement of our house and wrote. I didn't
always know why I wrote; I just knew I had to do it. I've been
writing ever since. When I write, I feel like I have a secret,
something that fortifies me, something that's all mine that
no one can take away from me. I feel I have something I owe
my life to, something that's bigger than me. When I write, I

become more alive, more whole in myself. It's a place where I am completely free to be myself. When I left home at an early age and my mother didn't know where I was or even if I was alive, my grandmother told her, "Don't worry. She's going to write it all down in her books." When poetry found me, when I was a young teen struggling to survive on my own, aching to know myself and be true to myself, writing became my path, my companion, my refuge. Not only did it save my life, but it was like finding out I was a witch who could write my own spells, spells that relieved my pain, spells that righted wrongs, spells that named what was hidden and shamed, spells that called my dreams to life. Through writing I found my voice and my power. I found my passion. I found where I belong.

## Why I Write

*I have never started a poem whose end I knew.*
*Writing a poem is discovering.*
— ROBERT FROST, "The Figure a Poem Makes"

When writing becomes your refuge and your companion, you will fight for it. When writing becomes your path, you will not let anyone or anything take it away from you. When writing becomes the medicine that heals your wounds, you will give it to yourself, you will make the time, you will do the discipline, you will find the words to name the unnameable. If writing has claimed you as its own, as it has me, you will know that writing is how we breathe, how we untangle, how we discover, and how we bloom from darkness into love.

INVITATION: Think about why you write. What calls and inspires you to write? Do you experience a kind of transformation when you write? Do you learn things about yourself you didn't know? How do you feel about yourself when you write? What happens for you when you suddenly find the right words to express what you think or feel? What is it like for you when you read back through a poem you've written?

 JUST WRITE! Why do you write? Keep asking yourself this question. Write down everything you hear yourself say. Don't judge or censor yourself. Answer yourself honestly. Dig deep. Find the answers. Find the questions. Allow yourself to be intense, funny, sad, passionate. Write it all down. Why do you write? What's in it for you? Where does it take you? What do you learn from writing? How does it change you? Why do you write?

## Example

### Why I Write — Meredith

I write to hear my own voice, because there are places of honesty and beauty that I go in my writing that I can't always go in my life, and I must, and because writing is where I grant safe passage to the shades of meaning that I don't always communicate to myself and others. When I write, I let the parts of me that hold my breath breathe. I write to let the light into my being and to let the darkness out. I write to release my pain and my past, to understand why and who I am, to savor my life by naming the ingredients that flavor my moments, and to celebrate my life in all its excruciating tenderness. I write to own myself, to capture the rhythms of my cycles: my journeys into the abyss and my travels through glory. I write to allow myself to feel, to climb inside my emotions and explore their reaches and textures. I write to summon my tears, to let them wash me hot and clean, then drain me, empty and free. I write myself alive and reborn. I write myself whole and holy. I write to experience myself transformed. I write because it involves me in this mysterious process of discovery, and because writing is a ritual whereby I create myself. I write to get naked and authentic, to delve into the marrow of my being where I make my blood. I write because I hurt and because I love. And so I won't lose anything. I write because I have always written and writing is how I know myself. I write because I am lonely and sensual and spiritual, and I need to make contact with the divine, and writing for me is like touching. It is rubbing and rolling my body against the divine until my boundaries dissolve and I no longer know where I start and where I stop, and I become part of the universe. I write to make myself eternal, to leave a piece of me stained into the ethers. I write because I believe God listens for the places where we love and own ourselves. I write to keep myself company. I write because I can't sleep, because I find the darkness at 3 a.m. electric and intoxicating, and writing is the way I communicate with that life energy. I write to grab onto the edge of shimmering chaos and ride it through lightning storms and come out stronger and clearer and a little bit crazier from having tasted the other side. I write to access my subconscious like a Ouija board, to learn things about myself I may not have known, and to make sure I master the things I'm learning. I write to make the world my own. I write to keep myself honest and to keep myself from watching TV. I write to keep my muse intrigued. I write because I can't draw.

• *Dig Deeper* •

Write about why you sing, dance, swim, bike, run, play a sport, make art, read, garden, play an instrument.

## Examples

*Why I Sing — Katie, 18*

I sing to feel alive and to break the chains from a time of numbness. I sing because to experience the pain, joy, aches, and wounds rush through my veins once more is infinitely better than feeling nothing at all. I sing to find a window into who I was and to explore the times when I felt most alive. I sing to find out who I can become, to relive memories, and restart myself. I sing to lose myself, to evaporate within a melody, only to unearth a new dimension of myself by singing and searching for the truth of a feeling. I sing to unleash my anger and fear and uncertainty through a searing line of melody that acts like a mighty wind blowing all that is poisonous from the purity that could be. I sing to connect, because if a word or even the tone of a syllable can evoke something real, then I have done my job. I sing so that I will be able to believe in something.

*Why I Play Volleyball — Mikayla, 11*

When I play volleyball
I forget about my size and my weight
and I just breathe and serve.
I feel good and happy.
I become a different person
less tense and more loose.
I feel the energy when my hand hits the ball
with such force that the other team knocks dead.
I feel the intensity of the other team rewind my mind.
The cheers of my team lift me up
and make me powerful.

## Write of Passage

*Come to the edge.*
*We might fall.*
*Come to the edge.*
*It's too high!*
*COME TO THE EDGE!*
*And they came*
*and he pushed*
*and they flew…*
— CHRISTOPHER LOGUE, "Come to the Edge"

In many indigenous cultures, the rite of passage ceremony marks important transitions from one life phase into another. These ceremonies are missing in our culture, and I feel this is a loss. Here are the ones I think need our acknowledgment: childhood to adolescence, adolescence to adulthood, menstruation, voice change, first kiss, first sexual experiences, graduation, college, living on your own, first job, first home, career change, major move, marriage, childbirth, divorce, middle age, menopause, a parent's death, a friend's death, the death of a spouse or partner, aging, elderhood, injury, illness, coming to terms with the end of our lives. Creating ceremony around a life transition is a powerful way to bring awareness, mark the occasion, share, and be witnessed. Invite friends, wear something beautiful, paint your face or body, go into nature, gather at night or wake up early for a sunrise ceremony, build a campfire or light candles, go to the ocean, a river, the forest. Dance and sing, cry and laugh, speak and write. Mark and celebrate this important life moment.

 INVITATION: Think about what phase of life you're in. What rite of passage would you like to acknowledge? Or perhaps there is one you never got to mark, grieve, or celebrate? What are you moving out of, and what are you moving into? How are you transforming, and who will you become?

 JUST WRITE! Choose a life transition, a current one or one from your past that you want to acknowledge. Create your own ceremony to mark this rite of passage. Write about what you do, what you learn, and how you feel. What wants to be grieved or honored? What wants to be birthed in you in this next phase of your life? What helps you speak your truth, claim your power, share your unique gifts, and know that you belong?

## Example

*Lady Crow — Raney, 12*

Midnight strands of silk blowing in the soft breeze.
Shining like a thousand ravens' feathers twisting and
    fluttering.
Thin braids speckle the hair, winding it like a river.

Nestled among the strands, two feathers.
One long and slender, striped with cream and oak,
it speckles and flashes, tattered and frayed, almost singed,
the other, a brilliant crimson with a wide plume.

This slender feather is one of the many tail feathers
of a young, speckled lady crow.
Her eyes bright and curious,
her sleek, soft feathers neatly arranged and flattened.
Her creamy, delicate head speckled
with dark stars of night
and a flat arrowhead beak.

And her tail.
Four of the famous tail feathers,
that give her the regal air of an eagle
and the daintiness of a chickadee.
She is a bird of power and destiny.

Only the girls with the deepest of souls
and the brightest of spirits
are awarded her feather.

The largest of the four is shed in late July
when strawberries burst and streams run clear.

This feather, my feather, one of the largest,
a sixteen-inch arrow of air and wind
floated down from the oldest of oak trees.
Collected by the girls of the trees and skies.
They hang for months until a girl is chosen.
A girl with fierce love and a kindling power within.

The feather is bestowed on her
a medallion hairpiece woven and knotted
until she too is one with the skies and the streams
the damp soil between her toes
the ocean of grasses and soft new shoots

She rises
her creamy face glowing
her striped feather shining
her hair glimmering
like a thousand crow feathers.

## Blindfold Walk

*Life is either a daring adventure, or nothing.*
— HELEN KELLER, *Let Us Have Faith*

Most of us depend on sight to get around in the world, and
we can easily take it for granted. Sight is a gift, but not having sight can teach us to see in new ways. Without sight we

have to draw on our other senses to give us cues and information. Without sight, our other senses develop a higher degree of sensitivity. I took a theater class once in which I was blindfolded for three hours. It was one of the most extraordinary experiences of my life. At first I was nervous and it was difficult to even walk. I just wanted to curl up in a corner and sleep, but I jumped in, and the experience changed my life. Detached from the sense of sight, my other senses came alive, and I experienced the world as a richly textured stew of sound, smell, taste, and touch. All my perceptions deepened. Sitting next to people, I could smell them, sense the subtle fluctuations in the tone of their voice, feel the heat or cool emanating from their skin as their mood changed. I learned to trust myself and others on a deeper level of knowing. I let go of my masks, found my true center, and felt like I understood others more clearly. I was reluctant to take the blindfold off. I didn't want to part with my newly awakened perception. When I did take it off, I was almost embarrassed. I felt I knew more than I was allowed to know about people and that I had revealed parts of myself I usually keep hidden. It was such a rich experience. I had no way of knowing that the things I learned from this experience would stay with me for so many years and inspire me to turn this into a writing invitation to share with my students.

 INVITATION: Get a sleep mask or a scarf that covers your eyes completely, or simply close your eyes for this experience. Do this with a friend or group.

Team up into groups of two. One person wears the blindfold. The other person is a helper. The key here is that the person with the blindfold is the leader. The blindfolded person can explore wherever they want, while the sighted person is simply making sure they don't get hurt, lost, or confused. You can do this either inside or outside. (If outside, make sure the blindfolded person is safe from traffic, cliffs, debris, and other potentially dangerous situations.) As the seeing person, you should stay in close contact with the blindfolded person at all times. You may need to hold the blindfolded person's hand until they relax and get comfortable moving around without their vision. You may also need to gently guide the blindfolded person away from areas where they could get hurt. The blindfolded person should take anywhere from fifteen minutes to an hour to explore and experience the world without sight. Keep talking to a minimum, unless needed to check in. Invite the blindfolded person to listen to their body and their feelings, to the sounds and smells around them. Afterward, switch roles so each of you gets to experience being blindfolded.

 JUST WRITE! Settle down in a quiet spot to reflect on and write about your experience. How is the world different without sight? How are you different? What did you notice? Which of your other senses came into play? How has this experience changed your outlook? How has it deepened your perceptions of yourself and others?

## Examples

*Blindfolded Walk — Mark, 17*

After the initial panic, after feeling paralyzed, alienated, and afraid to move, I relax into the darkness and find myself calm, balanced, and very much alive.

There is a spectrum of tones and inflection in every voice I hear, and though I've heard these voices a million times, they have never sounded quite like this before.

What is that smell? Sweet and spicy coming from the girl next to me. She is touching my hand, and my skin has a thousand satellite dishes ready to receive her message.

My own voice feels like it's coming out of a cave somewhere deep inside me, all I can do is trust that she's understood what I've said because I don't have the register of her facial expressions by which to gauge her reaction.

She is leading me gently by the arm, and I walk, unsure of my steps. I feel like there is something dark and shadowy just ahead of me, waiting for me to bump into it, but I never do. She lets go of my hand and I am on my own.

All I can do is trust my body to feel its way through the space and to move as though I know where I'm going. Where I am going?

She is putting something in my mouth. Oh my God! It is so sweet and juicy. It erupts as I chew it. I never knew a grape could be so succulent. I am smiling. Can I have more?

It's strange to smile when you can't see anybody smiling back at you. I feel suddenly alone and yet more deeply connected to myself and others than I ever imagined possible. Can we do this all day?

*Deeper Than My Eyes — Sarah, 16*

I thought I would feel uncomfortable wearing the blindfold.
I thought I would feel self-conscious and embarrassed.
But instead I felt completely centered, calm, free.
I never trusted myself to that degree before.
I didn't worry about what I look like
or what other people thought of me.
I simply listened inside myself
found a place of pure peace
saw myself with something
deeper than my eyes.

# • 16 •

# Carpe Diem

*How soon will we accept this opportunity*
*to be fully alive before we die?*
— STEPHEN LEVINE, *A Year to Live*

The fact that we exist is a mystery. Why we're here and where we go when we die is a mystery. While we're alive and aware of the short and precious gift of being, we can teach ourselves to make the kinds of choices that will allow us, at the end of our lives, to feel we lived in a meaningful way, that we contributed to others and the world, that we helped relieve suffering and, hopefully, that we encouraged joy, kindness, inspiration, and belonging. How do we celebrate this amazing life we've been given? How do we live today and each day with the knowledge that life is a fleeting gift? At the end of my life, I'd like to look back and feel that I have given my all and lived my life to the fullest, wouldn't you? I'd like to have few or no regrets when I die. The best way to do this is to get clear about what matters to us so we can make the choices that reflect our values and dreams. Each day is an opportunity to live fully. Carpe diem. Seize the day!

## Twenty-Four Hours to Live

A few years ago I took part in a Year to Live group, based on Stephen Levine's book *A Year to Live: How to Live This Year as If It Were Your Last*. Each of us committed to pretending that we had only one year left to live. We looked at each area of our life to see what we might do differently, knowing that our time was limited. It was a real wake-up call to stop procrastinating about my dreams, my joy, my love, and to live as fully as possible in every moment. I've shortened it here to twenty-four hours to help jump-start us into making choices from the awareness that life is NOW.

 INVITATION: Imagine you have twenty-four hours left to live. The why and how are not as important as what you do with this knowledge. How will you spend your last day? For ideas, read through the Questions for Your Last Day below.

 JUST WRITE! Starting now, you have twenty-four hours left to live. Write about how you feel and what is important to you. Address some or all of the following questions.

### • *Questions for Your Last Day* •

How do you spend your last day?
Who do you choose to be with?
What thoughts and feelings do you have?
What do you regret?

What are you most grateful for?
Who and what will you miss the most?
What do you want to be remembered for?

## Examples

*When I'm Gone — Billy, 16*

I'm sitting on the front porch, watching the sunrise. I'm the only one up. I'm dragging my family to the beach today, so I figure I'll let them sleep as long as they want. Birds are singing and the sun is starting to burn off the morning fog. I'm going to die today.

I wish I had loved more. I wish I hadn't been so hard on myself and my family. I wish I had traveled more, laughed more, sang more. So many hours I wasted watching TV. I could have been making friends, learning new things, exploring the world, kissing girls.

I wish I could take back all the times I yelled, all the times I lied, all the times I gave up. I promise today I will be kind to my family and friends. I will tell my mother I love her. I will praise my little sister. I will thank my father. I will hug and joke with my friends.

I see the ocean and the birds and the sky. I feel the sun on my face. We're having a picnic with all my favorite foods, and lots of ice cream. My dad is playing my favorite songs on the guitar. It seems like a regular Sunday, except today is my last day of life. I feel lucky to have lived.

*My Last Day — Michael, 17*

*Dawn*
You told me you like to dance
so I took you to the woods
and we chased each other between the trees
until you were out of breath
and fell to your knees laughing
I wanted to kiss you
but it was getting late
and when I turned around
you were gone.

*Dusk*
I had three small colored balls
that I would juggle at midnight
until they became too heavy to hold
and I dropped them on the floor
where they rolled under the table
out of sight.

*Night*
It's the neon tubes
that tell you
the convenience store
is OPEN!
It's foxfire
and stars
and bioluminescence
and an electric eel.
        *Goodbye*

## Butterfly Effect

*We ought to view ourselves with the same curiosity and openness with which we study a tree, the sky or a thought, because we too are linked to the entire universe.*

— Henri Matisse

One small action affects the whole. The dictionary defines *butterfly effect* as the phenomenon whereby a minute localized change in a complex system can have large effects elsewhere. Everything we do affects everything else, whether or not we're aware of it. We are part of a living matrix. The whole earth, and probably the whole cosmos, is alive and connected. We are not separate from it; indeed, we are an integral part of it. How can we live in a way that reflects this understanding and responsibility?

 INVITATION: With the butterfly effect in mind, imagine that turning over a beetle, killing an ant, breaking off a piece of coral reef, picking up trash, recycling and reusing, planting a garden, or helping a stranger can affect or even change the whole world.

 JUST WRITE! Write about one small action you take and how it affects your life, the earth, and the cosmos. Write about how everything is connected. Please make it something helpful, not destructive.

## Example

*Today I Picked Up a Seashell — Kate, 13*

It all started with the sky. To have a seashell, you need the
    sky.
The sky made the clouds and the clouds made the water.
There would be no ocean if there were no water.
When the ocean is done with the shell, it softly lays it on
    the sand.
And on that sand is a hand, ready to grab the shell when it
    comes.
We're staring at all of the earth's elements in one
    quarter-size item.
But where do you think that hand comes from?
Surely it did not appear from thin air!
No, this hand needs a human to cradle it.
And this human needs some food,
which needs the sun,
which all comes back to the sky.
Where does the beach come from?
Sand is just crushed-up rocks.
Those rocks come from volcanoes,
viciously spitting out hot lava.
These volcanoes need good soil and that soil needs water,
which we've already said comes from the clouds,
which come from the sky.
So my question is, how can something as violent as a
    volcano
turn into something as beautiful and calming as a seashell?

## Three Worldly Possessions

*In the end, only three things matter:*
*how much you loved, how gently you lived,*
*and how gracefully you let go of things not meant for you.*
— JACK KORNFIELD, *Buddha's Little Instruction Book*

All over the world natural disasters are happening: wild-fires, floods, earthquakes, tornadoes, hurricanes, tsunamis. Every day people lose their homes, their families, their pets, their possessions. These disasters are horrifying and traumatic, but through them, people often change their values for the better. They learn how resilient they are, they learn new ways to identify themselves, they find they can survive and live with less than they thought, they discover what they really need to survive, and in crisis, people drop the barriers of separation and rally together to help one another. What would it feel like to lose your home and your possessions? How would it change your view of yourself and the world? How would it change your values? If you had the chance to grab three items before you had to evacuate your home, what would you choose, and why?

 INVITATION: Imagine you are in an earthquake, a fire, a flood, or some other natural disaster. You have time to grab three items from your home before you need to flee. You might choose something useful, something sentimental, and something that brings help and comfort to you or others. For example, I choose a knife, my mother's necklace, and my guitar. What do you choose, and why?

JUST WRITE! Write about the three items you choose to take, and why. How does imagining this experience change the way you think about who you are, what you value, your relationship with material possessions, your resourcefulness, and what you really need to survive?

## Example

*What Matters? — Norah, 14*

House is shaking.
It's an earthquake!
Time slows down.
I look around.
What matters?
What to grab?
What is all this stuff in my house?
I don't really need any of it
and yet somehow, I need all of it.
What matters?
What to grab?

My stuffed zebra, my tarot cards
my down comforter, my journal
my sewing machine, my art supplies
my plants, my flute, my paintings
my mother's ring, my favorite boots?
What matters?
What to grab?
Some invisible clock
is ticking away the seconds

to the tune of doomsday.
What matters?
What to grab?

My backpack with my laptop for communication
My flute to calm me and others
A box of energy bars to eat
and to feed others who are hungry.

I'm lucky to get out alive.
It doesn't matter what I grab.
What matters is my life,
my family, my friends.

## Carpe Diem

*How we spend our days is, of course, how we spend our lives.*
— ANNIE DILLARD, *The Writing Life*

How do you spend your days? Are you tapping your potential? Are you engaging your unique brilliance and love? Are you using your capabilities and nurturing your passions? Do you make time to play music, go for a walk, spend quality time with friends and family, work for a cause you believe in, learn something new? Or are you waiting for life to choose you?

 INVITATION: Consider each of the Life Areas listed below, and be honest with yourself about which areas need more attention for you to live more fully. Be specific about how to nurture your dreams, starting now.

JUST WRITE! For each life area below, write a few words or lines about what you can do to cultivate this part of your life so it brings you greater fulfillment and purpose.

**Life Areas:** Work, career, school, family, friends, community, personal growth, love relationships, fun, communication, creativity, health, exercise, service, spirituality, education, travel, adventure. Feel free to add your own.

## Example

*Today's the Day — Ethan, 17*

Today's the day I fight the beast and win
Today's the day I bust the chains that hold me back
and climb out of the cave toward the sun
Today's the day I am stronger
than the quicksand of my doubt
Today's the day when I take the horses
named fear and dreams
and hold the reins in my hands
until they become power,
my power.

Today's the day I reach beneath my sadness
and find my heart
Today it doesn't matter what anyone else thinks of me
what matters is what I think of me
Today I am willing to be seen
to stand up in front of my class
and read my poem

even though I keep my hood on
and the sound of my own voice surprises me.

Today's the day I say my name out loud
I look in the mirror
I make a choice
to believe in myself.

# • 17 •

# Attitude of Gratitude

*It is not joy that makes us grateful;*
*it is gratitude that makes us joyful.*
— BROTHER DAVID STEINDL-RAST,
*Gratefulness, the Heart of Prayer*

Neuroscientists tell us that spending a few minutes each day in gratitude rewires our brain and our mood for peace and joy. Try it. It works! I had insomnia for eighteen years after a car accident, and one of the things that finally helped me to sleep again was to write a gratitude list every night for three years. This put me in my heart and took me out of the anxiety loop in my head. Writing about what we're grateful for, from the apple we had for lunch to the people we love, reminds us that we have what we need, that we're cared for and safe, that there is goodness in our lives, and that we belong. Yes, we struggle, this is part of life and growing, but we can choose to focus on what helps us to feel good about ourselves and our lives, and this makes life so much more enjoyable. Gratitude helps!

INVITATION: Read through the Categories of Gratitude list below and think about all the things and all the people in each area of your life that you appreciate, from the smallest to the most important. We can get so busy, tired, and distracted that we forget all the people and things that help make our lives possible, special, and meaningful. You'll be amazed at how focusing on what you're grateful for can change your mood and help you feel better.

**Categories of Gratitude:** Friends, family, work, school, relationships, feelings, memories, health, safety, home, pets, music, nature, exercise, favorite foods, hobbies, activities, belongings, holidays, seasons, upcoming events. Add your own!

 JUST WRITE! Write a list of all the people and things you're grateful for. Include everything that adds to your well-being and happiness, from the smallest to the biggest. I encourage everyone to keep a gratitude list.

## Example

*Grateful — Aiden, 15*

My best friend
My parents
Trees and animals
Honeybees
Clean air to breathe
Clean water to drink
Sunshine
Strong body

New girlfriend
Acing my science exam
My new bike
Summertime

### *Ho'oponopono*

*I'm sorry. I forgive you. Thank you. I love you.*

When I lived in Hawaii, I learned a powerful healing tool called *Ho'oponopono*. This is the Hawaiian wisdom way for making things right with ourselves and others. The Hawaiian word *Ho'oponopono* comes from *ho'o* (to make) and *pono* (right). When we repeat the word *pono*, it means "doubly right" or being right with both yourself and others. It boils down to apologizing, forgiving, appreciating, and loving one another.

*Ho'oponopono* has four parts:

**Apology:** I'm sorry; please forgive me.
**Forgiveness:** I forgive you.
**Gratitude:** Thank you.
**Love:** I love you.

 INVITATION: If you think about it, these are the only four things we ever really need to say to someone. And while they seem short and sweet, each phrase is power packed. Some of them are easy to feel and say. Others take more work. We can apply these phrases to ourselves. Think about the ways you harm yourself by punishing and abandoning yourself and the ways you help yourself by acknowledging and accepting yourself. Now think about the people in your life. Which of these phrases do you most need to say, and to whom? Which ones are hard to say, and which are easy? You can even say or write these phrases to people in your life who have passed. Practice saying all of them to yourself and others: I'm sorry. I forgive you. Thank you. I love you.

 **JUST WRITE!** Start by writing a letter to yourself, using each of the four phrases. What can you apologize to yourself for, forgive yourself for, thank yourself for, and love yourself for? Be specific. Really take the time to give yourself the healing medicine of each one. Next, write a list of the most important people in your life, the people you are closest to or the people with whom you've had your share of struggles. See which of the four phrases is the most needed to bring peace and resolution to this relationship. Trust me, you'll know! Write a poem to this person telling them you're sorry, forgiving them and asking them to forgive you, thanking them, or letting them know you love them. Finally, see if you can address all four of these phrases to this person. After you've written the poem, you can keep it, burn it, throw it away, or give it to the person you wrote it to.

## Examples

*Apology — Elizabeth, 14*

I am sorry for all the lies
that were in disguise
this life don't always play nice
I am sorry for all the fights
during the cold nights

but sometimes my hands were tied
That's not an excuse
I am sorry
I lied.


*To My Sister — Rachel, 15*

I'm sorry
your anger
my silence

I'm sorry
your need
my distance

I'm sorry
your order
my chaos

I'm sorry
your broken
my open


*Thank You — Natalia, 19*

When I knocked on your door at 3 a.m.
wet from rain and tears
and you took me in
with hot soup
and a soft blanket
and you listened
and you didn't judge me

and in the morning
you put my hands in the garden
and I pulled up fistfuls
of wild strawberries
like tiny beating hearts.


*My Way of Saying — Thomas, 16*

Down in the basement
of my heart
what I want to say to you
is caught
in cobwebs and dust
boxes ready to bust
never opened
never closed
is this the life we chose?
This is my way of saying,
I forgive you.


*I Love You — Ally, 16*

I love you
hair tangled
eyes shining
boots caked in mud
always late
always hungry
always a present
in your pocket.

## • 18 •

# Wildly Alive

*It began in mystery, and it will end in mystery, but what a savage and beautiful country lies in between.*
— DIANE ACKERMAN, *A Natural History of the Senses*

This is it! This is your life! NOW. You don't get another chance. This is not a dress rehearsal. You think you have lots of time, but it goes fast. Your most important job is to be wildly alive by creating a life you love. Figure out what rocks your world, and do it. Find a way to share what you're passionate about. Happiness is an inside job. It usually walks hand in hand with purpose. You're responsible for creating a life worth living. This life is a mystery, and we are part of that mystery. Why are we here? How did all this life come into being? Stay open. Be curious. Ask questions. Choose experiences that help you learn and grow. Know yourself. Be true to yourself. Be kind to others. Dream big, and make it happen!

## Gardens and Graveyards

*The things we bury can tell you a lot about who we are.*
*The only difference between a garden and a graveyard*
*is what we choose to put in the soil.*

— RUDY FRANCISCO, "The Heart and the Fist"

Imagine your life is a big grassy field. This field is divided into two parts, a garden and a graveyard. One is for planting things and growing, and the other is for burying things and letting go. What to grow and what to dump? Think about which of your qualities go to which place. Nothing is lost; everything is part of learning. What you bury in the graveyard will eventually become compost for your garden. Our mistakes become the seeds of our wisdom.

 INVITATION: Think about which qualities in you it's time to let go of and bury, to turn back into compost and soil. Think about which qualities in you you'd like to plant in your garden and nurture, so they grow and blossom.

 JUST WRITE! Write a list of the qualities you're ready to let go of and bury. Write a list of the qualities you want to nurture and grow. Use these lists to write a poem about what you bury in your graveyard and what you plant in your garden. Dig deep. Turn the soil.

## Example

*My Garden — Liza, 14*

I'm burying doubt and depression
I'm planting self-confidence and gratitude
I'm burying saying yes when I mean NO!
I'm planting being true to myself
I'm burying worrying about my weight
I'm planting celebrating my body
I'm burying whining about things
I'm planting making shit happen
I'm burying skinny jeans
I'm planting sweatpants
I'm burying watching TV
I'm planting playing the piano
I'm burying hiding
I'm planting being seen
I'm burying needing others to acknowledge me
I'm planting knowing my own value
I'm burying holding grudges
I'm planting acceptance and understanding
I'm burying punishing myself
I'm planting learning from my mistakes
I'm burying the old me that was too small
I'm planting the new me with room to grow
I can take up as much space as I want
because I matter!

## Breathe In and Breathe Out

Here's a twist on the way we usually huff and puff to exhale and rid ourselves of a bad feeling. There's an ancient Buddhist practice called Tonglen, introduced to the West by Buddhist nun Pema Chödrön. It goes like this: instead of forcefully breathing out what is uncomfortable, such as our anger or frustration, we breathe in what is uncomfortable, we feel it, and then we transmute it into peace and breathe it out to ripple through the web of life. What I love about this practice is that it teaches us that we have the power to change what we're feeling, that we don't have to be pushed around by our feelings, that we have choice, and that we need not identify with feelings that ultimately make us ill. Let's give it a try in writing.

 INVITATION: Get in touch with an uncomfortable feeling such as anger, fear, hurt, frustration. Put your hand on your heart, breathe in the challenging feeling, and say, "I am here with you." Stay with it until it softens, changing into a feeling of calm peace. Consciously exhale this peace into the world, knowing this feeling is now rippling through you and through the web of life.

 JUST WRITE! Start with the words *I breathe in*, followed by anything that is hard, challenging, uncomfortable, unconscionable. On the next line down, write the words *I breathe out*, followed by anything that brings you a feeling of peace, love, hope. Try addressing topics that are personal, societal, political, global.

## Example

*Breathe In, Breathe Out — Ashtyn, 9*

I breathe in a hot spicy fireball
I breathe out a cold flowing stream

I breathe in an angry cat
I breathe out a cuddled cat

I breathe in screaming from frustration with school
I breath out birdsong full of sweetness

I breathe in scratching cat claws
I breathe out the soft tickle of my mom's fingers on my neck

I breathe in frozen tears
I breathe out melted honey

I breathe in slamming doors
I breathe out soft whispers

I breathe in witches cackling in my nightmares
I breathe out a fire that wraps around me like a golden
    bubble

I breathe in soggy pizza
I breathe out rainbow balloons

## Birthday Wish

*You get in life what you have the courage to ask for.*
— OPRAH WINFREY

Asking for what you want is a powerful practice. The more you learn to ask for what you really want, the better chance you have of getting it. What do you wish for when you blow out the candles on your birthday cake? Why do we make these wishes silently? I wish we would make them out loud so everyone could know what we want.

 INVITATION: Imagine it's your birthday and whatever you wish for will come true. The trick is, you have to ask out loud — and be specific!

 JUST WRITE! Write a poem asking for exactly what you want.

## Example

*Birthday Wishes — Casey, 16*

For quiet so I can hear myself think
For understanding from my parents, sister, and teachers
For more hours in the day and more sleep in the morning
For a way to express all this energy I feel
For the grown-ups to stop killing the earth

For me and my friends to make music that heals the world
For people to stop fighting each other
For school to be done so I can live my life the way I want
For more friends who want to change the world with me

## Love Yourself Up!

You may think loving yourself is easy. But I bet you put it off. I sure did. Why is it so hard to be kind to ourselves? Why do we love others but struggle to love ourselves? Many of us search outside ourselves our whole lives to fill the holes and emptiness we feel inside. But when we learn to love ourselves and to treat ourselves with kindness, we find that we belong to ourselves and to life, and it's this belonging we have been waiting for our whole lives. Loving ourselves is the key to wholeness. It takes practice. Let's start now.

 INVITATION: Think about all the things you love about yourself. Be willing to accept yourself in all your perfect imperfection. Think about the challenges you've faced or are facing now and how you've learned and grown from them. Be kind to yourself. We're all here to learn. We're human. Being human is enough. Being human is plenty. Give yourself the love you deserve.

 JUST WRITE! Write a love letter to yourself. Hold nothing back. Love yourself up! If you need to pretend the letter is from someone else, that's fine. Just write it!

## Example

*Now I Love Myself — Lexi, 18*

I love myself
my ocean eyes
my moonlit skin
my heart of fire

I love myself
but I didn't always

You probably don't know
that I spent years
climbing through bogs of depression
clawing through quicksand of self-loathing
struggling with such massive insecurity
I could not leave the house

I love myself
but I didn't always

I'm not perfect
I have a lot to learn
but now I stand up tall
now I feel proud of who I am
now I love myself.

## How to Be a Poet

*Celebrate every gorgeous moment.*
— SARK, "How to Be an Artist"

Yes, you are now a poet! Being a poet is a way of life. For most of us, it means being deeply and wildly alive. It means being true to ourselves. It means giving ourselves passionately to everything we do, experiencing life fully, honoring the depth of our perception and sensitivity. It means taking big bites of life but also allowing for quiet reflection. Being a poet is finding a lifeline in writing. We thrive on experiences that move and inspire us and make us need to write. So it's important to know what these are. What moves and inspires you? What makes you feel deeply? What makes you need to write? Once we get a taste of how good it feels when our writing flows, when we're inspired and in the zone, then the challenge is how to keep it flowing. How do we stay tuned to our inspiration channel? How do we keep the door open? How do we keep our muse singing in our ear? For this invitation, I'm borrowing from author and artist SARK and her glorious piece "How to Be an Artist."

 INVITATION: Think about all the things you do that inspire the poet in you. Think about the things that move you, thrill you, make you feel deeply, connect you to yourself and others, and make you feel alive!

**JUST WRITE!** Write a list of what puts you in a poetic mood. What gets your juices flowing? What helps you feel inspired? What makes you want or need to write? Promise yourself you'll do at least one of these things every day.

## Example

*How to Be a Poet — Nathan, 15*

Listen to your inner voice
Have mood swings
Abandon reality
Walk in the rain
Live in the now
Travel everywhere
Lie in the grass
Sing at the top of your lungs
Don't believe everything you hear
Keep your thoughts flowing
Feel everything
Don't be afraid
Talk to the trees
Say what's on your mind
Get angry
Stay up all night
Cook dinner for your friends
Wear old boots
Be relaxed
Love or hate everything

Be spontaneous
Spend time alone
Write down everything
Don't judge yourself
Kiss someone you love
Eat chocolate-chip ice cream
Sleep outside
Laugh a lot & cry a lot
Know how to listen
Take midnight walks

## • *Dig Deeper* •

Write about how to be an athlete, a philosopher, an artist, a musician — anything that celebrates and honors who you are!

## Example

*How to Be a Thinker — Kate, 8*

Stargaze and make memory constellations
When it rains, visit the mildew in the morning
The unknown is your happy place
Puddles are for jumping
A book is not an assignment, it's an adventure
Rename things
Fill your passport with stamps, not your house with stuff
Nighttime is for partying, not for sleeping
Animals are healing
Forests are for wandering, not for listening to your guide
A thermos holds many things
Bath bombs are a necessity

Let a seaplane skim the thoughts of your mind
Get wet
Think miniature

## Wildly Alive

*Poetry is a matter of life, not just a matter of language.*
— Lucille Clifton,
as quoted by Mickey Pearlman in *Listen to Their Voices*

What does it feel like to be wildly alive? Imagine yourself open, in touch with who you are, true to yourself, full of feeling, expressive, living a life you love. What is the most amazing version of you and your life you can imagine? If you were telling a friend the story of your dream life, what would you say? If you could create exactly what you want, what would it be? What does it look like and feel like to be wildly, unashamedly, powerfully alive? Can you imagine a life in which you do the very things every day that bring you joy and purpose? How do you share your talents, skills, and passion to help others? What we believe and imagine about ourselves, we become. Believe in yourself! You have permission to be wildly alive!

 INVITATION: Close your eyes and imagine yourself two or three or five years from now. How do you feel about yourself and your life? What kind of work do you do? Where do you live? What are your interests and hobbies? Who are your friends and family? Do you have a pet? How do you spend your time? What's important to you? What do you value? Are you learning something new? How do you contribute to your family, friends, community, world? What's the best possible life you can imagine for yourself, a life that makes you feel wildly alive, proud of yourself, and that you're contributing something meaningful to the world?

 JUST WRITE! Write the details of your dream life. Include everything you can think of that helps you to feel happy and fulfilled. What you can imagine, you can become. Writing is a creative act. Create a life worth living.

## Example

*This Is My Life! — Cara, 18*

In five years from now
I'm brave
I shave my head
I get a tattoo
a Celtic knot
on my left forearm
with the words
*Choose Love*
tangled in gold
through the knot.

My best friend is my Irish wolfhound, Oz
as in The Wizard

He's big and dashing and mischievous
He never takes no for an answer
Oz has more friends than I do
He introduced me to my boyfriend!

I live in Telluride, Colorado
I'm a ski instructor
Every day I fly down slopes of white powder
I carve my signature in the fresh canvas of snow
a spray of rainbow crystals shining all around me
like a halo
Every day I watch people's faces
light up like the sun.

My heart is happy.
My body is alive.
My mind is at peace.
This is my life!

# Speak Your Truth, Even If Your Voice Shakes!

*Poetry [is] more necessary than ever*
*as a fire to light our tongues.*

— NAOMI SHIHAB NYE, *Salting the Ocean*

This is the part of your journey where you get to choose whether or not to share your poems with other people. It took me a very long time to have the confidence to share mine. I hope you don't wait as long as I did. What I found was that even though I was nervous and my hands and voice shook and I wanted to run away, and that even though I could barely remember my name, let alone my poem, when I read my poetry to others, I became more alive, more whole. I claimed myself. I allowed myself to be witnessed in my strength and my vulnerability, in all the beautiful mess of who I am, and it helped me learn that I am human. And being human is enough; it is perhaps more than enough.

When I share my poetry, there are always people who cry and cheer, and I know that everything I've been through and write about is universal and that voicing it is cathartic not only for me but for others. People thank me. They say I put the things they feel into the words they could not find and that it heals them to hear those words. When you commune with your own being and touch your own truth, it saves you. Sharing your truth with others is powerful medicine. Our poems are our pearls. We take what hurts and make it into something beautiful that has the power to heal us and others.

If you choose to share your poems, you may feel nervous and afraid. It's okay to feel nervous and afraid. It means you're alive. Yes, it's uncomfortable, but you won't die from it. We're more afraid to feel fear than we are afraid of whatever we're doing. Allow yourself to feel afraid. It's natural. Make friends with your fear. Say hello to your fear. I like to talk to my fear. I say, *I know you're scared, but you're welcome here. We're allowed to be afraid. We're allowed to make mistakes. We're allowed to be exactly who we are. Take my hand and I'll take yours, and here we go!* Allow your fear and nervousness to give you energy. Your hands and voice may shake, but I promise you, after you read, you will feel like you're on fire. You will feel wildly alive, because you are!

You can start by sharing your poems with friends or family; then try sharing with a small group or class. The more you do it, the better you get and the more comfortable you feel. Perhaps there's an arena at your school, community center, or local coffeehouse where you can do a poetry reading. Perhaps you know other people who write poems and would like a place to share their work too. Once you feel more comfortable, try an open-mic poetry reading at a larger venue. This is a great way to connect with other poets.

You may want to submit your poetry to some online

poetry magazines. It's fun and encouraging to receive the acknowledgment of getting your work published. Just be prepared to get lots of rejections. I did. Don't be discouraged. Editors are very picky and are usually looking for a specific theme or style. If your poems don't get accepted, it doesn't mean they're not good. Try again. Also, remember, don't write what you think others want. Write for yourself. Write the poems that you feel good about, the ones where you dig deep, the ones that save your life and set you free.

You can also make your own book. I've had friends create artful homemade books with handmade paper and a typewriter. Make a bunch of these and give them as gifts. Or self-publish with online companies that help you create, print, and promote your book.

 INVITATION: Think about what motivates you to share your poetry with others and what blocks you. What feelings arise when you think about sharing your poems?

 JUST WRITE! Complete the following statements to help you welcome and make peace with the seemingly contradictory yet coexisting emotions of fear, panic, anxiety, desire, excitement, and empowerment you may feel when you consider sharing your poetry with others.

The biggest thing I'm afraid of when sharing my poetry is...
The reason I want to share my poetry is...
When I share my poetry I feel...

To share or not to share your poetry is your choice. You'll know if and when you're ready. Sometimes writing is enough. Sometimes the call to share is as loud as the call to write. Believe in yourself and your poetry. Trust your rhythms. Take chances. Dig deep. Follow what makes you hum. Remember, you're part of the great mystery and web of life. Be curious. Be kind. Be grateful. You're human, and being human is plenty. I hope this book and your poetry help you to love yourself and your life.

# Love and Gratitude

Huge thanks to Patrick Miller, my agent and now friend at Fearless Literary, who came across my essay in *Common Ground* and asked if I had a book to write! My mother, for believing in magic and believing in me. Annelies Atchley, my best friend. Steven Adler, true-blue. Susanne Paynovich, Mermaid Queen. Susan Wooldridge, word wizard and new friend. California Poets in the Schools. Marc Allen, Georgia Hughes, and the team at New World Library for helping me share my journey and the lifesaving power of poetry writing. And to my students, who always amaze and inspire me with their courage and creativity. The example poems in this book were written and shared with permission by kids from all walks of life whom I have had the honor of teaching over the past thirty years. They are brilliantly brave and creative, and I hope they stay true to their art, their hearts, and their voices.

# About the Author

Meredith Heller is a poet, singer-songwriter, and educator with degrees in writing and education. She studied in the graduate departments of Johns Hopkins University, Naropa University, and Goddard College. She is the author of three poetry collections: *Songlines*, *River Spells*, and *Yuba Witch*. A California Poet in the Schools, she teaches workshops for grades 1 to 12 in public and private schools, in the Creative Writing Department at Marin School of the Arts, in Juvenile Hall, and nationally on Zoom for kids and adults. She is part of the Kennedy Center's Teaching Artists Present program, contributing her original poetry lessons to their online video library. Her writing appears in *Rebelle Society*, *We'Moon*, *Raw Earth Ink*, *Quiet Lightning*, *Tiny Seed*, *The Aquarian*, *Avocet*, *Common Ground*, *Tiny House*, and *American Songwriter*. A nature girl who spent fifteen summers solo backpacking, she hikes the trails daily and lives in a tiny cottage in Marin County, California. She spends her summers camping and writing. For info about her poetry workshops on Zoom, visit www.meredithheller.com.